WHEN PAY PLANS GO WRONG

Managing Compliance Issues *Before* the Audit

Jude Sotherlund

Acknowledgments

WorldatWork would like to acknowledge the following individuals for contributing to the completion of this book:

Technical Reviewers

Sean D. Delaney
NCR Corporation

Mary E. Hall, CCP
Total Compensation Services Inc.

Lorrie M. Ferraro, CCP, PHR
Parexel International

John A. Rubino, CCP, CBP, GRP
Rubino Consulting Services

WorldatWork Staff Contributors

Dan Cafaro

Betty Laurie

Maggie Conners

Barry Oleksak

Rebecca Williams Ficker

WorldatWork®

**The Professional Association for
Compensation, Benefits and Total Rewards**

WorldatWork is the world's leading not-for-profit professional association dedicated to knowledge leadership in compensation, benefits and total rewards. Founded in 1955, WorldatWork focuses on disciplines associated with attracting, retaining and motivating employees. In addition to providing professional affiliation, WorldatWork offers highly acclaimed certification (CCP®, CBP™ and GRP®) and education programs, the monthly *workspan®* magazine, online information resources, surveys, publications, conferences, research and networking opportunities.

WorldatWork
14040 N. Northsight Blvd., Scottsdale, AZ 85260
480/951-9191 • Fax 480/483-8352 • www.worldatwork.org

© 2003 WorldatWork
ISBN: 1-57963-129-0

Author Acknowledgments

Writing a manuscript that succinctly captures the complexities of compensation has not been easy. As an analyst, I found it hard, at times, to put my finger on the most important or cogent facts. For encouraging me to do so — even when others said, "no one cares," "it's too difficult," or "I'm trying to figure out how to escape such liability"— I am eternally grateful to my husband, Dana. His sound analytic skills and advice to "keep it simple" and "make the case" were invaluable. May our children grow up working toward justice and fairness in life, as they do now on the playground.

Over the years, I have benefited, both personally and professionally, from the advice and counsel of many in both the public and private sectors. To those in the public sector serving at the Equal Employment Opportunity Commission and the U.S. Department of Labor: Continue to carry out the public trust with fairness and flexibility. To my colleagues in the private sector trying to navigate the waters of pay equity: Stay the course. To the many who have shared their personal situations and professional dilemmas with me: You have my gratitude as your confidence in me gave me the fortitude to pursue this end.

Many individuals have been instrumental in this book reaching final fruition. A special thanks goes out to my editor, Dan Cafaro, who saw merit in this undertaking right from the start and to Cari Dominguez, who continues to champion the cause of inclusion and equity in employment. To the many who gave freely of their time to read excerpts, you have my appreciation, especially Alan Roddy, Maria Korn, Rene Henry and Tania Muskett for having reviewed the manuscript in its entirety. Last, but not least, my admiration and appreciation to my parents, Jim and Ursula, who raised all 10 of us in an equal opportunity household.

Table of Contents

Chapter 5: Broadbanding — The Present and the Future? 71

Preface

"You are now the keeper of the family jewels." Those were the words that welcomed me, earlier in my career, as I assumed my new role which included directing the executive compensation and executive benefits functions at a major financial services institution. And even though my new role entailed other duties, such as executive staffing and succession planning, by far, executive compensation consumed most of our attention and resources.

I learned a lot from that experience. I learned about employers' fear of defection by their key executives. Such defection would involve not only the loss of precious talent but also the abduction of intellectual property, a key competitive asset in today's marketplace. I also learned about the strong emotional association that employees make between their pay and their self-worth. For employees, compensation is personal. It is not only about one's pay, it is also about one's worth in the eyes of an employer; thus, the constant need to prove one's uniqueness — "unique qualifications," "unique experiences," or being "uniquely positioned." These and other similar dynamics make well-conceived, highly rational pay plans vulnerable to the constant intrusion of subjective, irrational acts.

Family jewels are closely guarded, and so are compensation data. I learned that I was to use the "need to know" litmus test to share information with other functions. If my colleagues in other functional areas, such as EEO or staffing, couldn't make a compelling case for access to the compensation data, the request was denied. Except for retained outside compensation consultants operating under "attorney-client privileges," members of the executive management committee or select board members, the "need to know" threshold was rarely, if ever, met. Fear of piracy by competitors, fear of liability or, worse, fear of causing employee unrest, conspired to generate a pay sensitive culture, with some dysfunctional consequences.

A few years later, I had the privilege of joining the administration of the 41st U.S. President, George H.W. Bush, as a political appointee in the U.S. Department of Labor. I was appointed by the then Secretary of Labor,

Elizabeth Dole, to serve as Director of the Office of Federal Contract Compliance Programs (OFCCP), which is the agency responsible for auditing and monitoring the employment policies and practices of federal contractors to ensure nondiscrimination and diversity in the workplace. With Secretary Dole's support, the OFCCP launched an unprecedented initiative: the Glass Ceiling Initiative, designed to identify and remove workplace barriers affecting the advancement of women and people of color into upper level jobs. Jude Sotherlund, also serving as a political appointee at the time, was a lead member of the glass ceiling task force that launched this initiative. Her findings and contributions were fundamental to the success of this initiative, an initiative that has transcended administrations and continues to sustain its relevance to this day.

While conducting our glass ceiling audits, we met with corporate executives, analyzed data and interviewed human resources managers. It soon became quite evident that the lack of access to compensation data by EEO managers and others charged with ensuring nondiscrimination in employee rewards systems was a serious impediment to their efforts to fully carry out their responsibilities. In all instances, we discovered that these individuals had no access to information on bonus or long-term compensation awards, thus rendering them powerless to conduct any meaningful comparative analyses. Such lack of collaborative, information sharing efforts continues, more often than not, to this day.

Two other career experiences affirm the need for the type of practical, insightful guidance contained in this book. More recently, my six years of experience as a director and partner at two major international search firms revealed a need for greater oversight and checks and balances in the preparation and negotiation of employment offers. For some, negotiating a compensation package is more of a sport than a process. Individuals are rated on their negotiation skills. Limits are tested. How else can one justify "buying out" one person's pension from another company and not another's? Why else would one person command a sign-on bonus equivalent to one year's pay and not another? Unfortunately, those more likely to receive a lesser offer are those who haven't had much practice or exposure to the negotiations game, namely women and people of color.

Today, I have the honor of serving as chair of the U.S. Equal Employment Opportunity Commission, the agency responsible for enforcing the Equal Pay Act and Title VII of the Civil Rights Act, in addition to other statutes. Many of the situations that I have witnessed in the past have come to a head right here, at the Commission, with multi-million dollar settlements for disparate pay practices and other forms of discrimination. Even after almost 40 years of enforcing civil rights employment law, discrimination is alive and well. That is why a thorough discussion of fairness and equity in compensation practices can be a useful tool for ensuring compliance with the law.

In her book, *When Pay Plans Go Wrong*, Jude Sotherlund has captured and skillfully analyzed the organizational players and perspectives that, potentially, hold the key to conquering, as she puts it, the "final frontier": income equity. Yet, without teamwork, coordination and collaboration across functions, this final frontier may elude Corporate America. *When Pay Plans Go Wrong* lays out the business case for financial fairness and places the responsibility for ensuring it squarely on the shoulders of the people leading organizations. Plans are inanimate. It is the people behind the plans that can make a difference, if they work together toward a common goal. This book provides a blueprint for making it happen. Now it is up to the people.

— *Cari M. Dominguez, CCP*

Introduction

D ocumentaries, articles and entire books are dedicated to the changes that America has experienced in the 20th century — her achievements and her failures. Unequivocally, she has come a long way in a relatively short span of time.

These profound changes are characterized in part by the influx of women that entered America's work force in the 1940s. As the nation turned its attention to the health and education of its children, the federal government introduced child labor laws that limited hours and defined work conditions, and other laws that regulated formal schooling. Workplaces gradually evolved into safer and more flexible environments, while working conditions improved considerably. In turn, the nation's work force became more inclusive, offered various career options and provided more choices for employees seeking a work/life balance.

Chief among these changes has been the enormous gains in work force advancement for people of color and women. An unprecedented amount of women now work outside the home and in nontraditional jobs, and an increasing number of women and minorities have reached mid- and senior-level management in corporate America. Women and members of minority groups also have achieved Cabinet-level positions within the U.S. government, hold seats on the U.S. Supreme Court and directly serve the U.S. president.

However, no matter how far women and people of color advance in their professions, they are not fully participating in the American dream until they are paid equitably. Income inequity remains one of the final hurdles to workplace equity. Intervention and accountability — in the form of sound policies and practices — will ensure that employment compensation — in all its many forms — is fair, flexible and free of discriminatory bias. While good management practices yield *differentiation* in compensation, poor practices or bias lead to *discrimination*. The latter should be eradicated.

1

Framing the Issue
of Workplace Inequity

"Discrimination is still a reality, even when it takes different forms. Instead of Jim Crow, there is racial redlining and profiling. Instead of 'separate but equal,' there is separate and forgotten."

— George W. Bush,
*speaking at the 2000 National Association
for the Advancement of Colored People annual convention*

A cting as a clarion call to demographers, public policy analysts and politicians in 1987, the publication of *Workforce 2000: Work and Workers for the 21st Century* heightened awareness that America's work force indeed was about to change drastically.

"Almost two-thirds of the new entrants into the work force between now and the year 2000 will be women, and 61 percent of all women of working age are expected to have jobs by the year 2000."

This assertion caught the attention of all. The report continued, "Minorities will be a larger share of the new entrants into the labor force … Immigrants will represent the largest share of the increase in population and the work force since the First World War."[1]

Management nationwide went into a tailspin. HR professionals were inundated with queries and concerns. Many spent the 1990s preparing for this changing work force. *Would my company have to change its corporate policies? Would we have to change our corporate culture? How should we integrate this new work force?*

Emergence of Diversity: Affirmative Efforts of the 1990s

For many large employers, the 1990s brought enlightenment. Diversity, a buzzword to describe the many faces of the proposed new work force, came to have vastly divergent definitions. *Does it include me? Does it include him? Or her?* In short, many refer to diversity as those human qualities that are different from our own and those of the group to which we belong. This encompasses ethnicity, race, gender and other human characteristics.

How does diversity differ from Equal Employment Opportunity (EEO), nondiscrimination or affirmative action concepts? Equal employment opportunity refers to one's legal responsibility to *not* discriminate against people of color, women and other protected groups in hiring, training and development; promotions; discharge; compensation; and other employment practices. Affirmative action in an employment setting means that legally an employer should affirmatively broaden the net, reach out and proactively attempt to include these same protected groups in his/her employment practices. Both have a basis in law. Diversity does not.

Perhaps for this very reason, diversity was more palatable than equal employment or affirmative action and received executive backing and financial support. Diversity consultants appeared overnight to help management address the concerns that these new entrants might bring. Diversity became part of mission statements, business plans and strategic goals. Diversity consultants almost always recommended training of the work force ... as many people as possible.

To some, sitting through diversity training was enlightening. For others, it meant nothing more than good management techniques with a little extra vigilance. And others only "did diversity" at the time and place required. Many in the corporate ranks cheered diversity endeavors — particularly people of color, women, single parents and individuals with disabilities. Others cringed every time they heard the word. For this latter group, diversity meant catering to people different than themselves.

Call it timing, a coincidence or a result of the heightened awareness that diversity training brought, but people of color and women made many strides in the workplace in the 1990s. Individuals with disabilities found many doors previously closed being opened and greater accommodations being made.

We can attribute much of this headway to new laws and greater law enforcement by the Equal Employment Opportunity Commission (EEOC) and the U.S. Department of Labor's Office of Federal Contract Compliance Programs (OFCCP). These enforcement bodies opened many a door for the disabled and "nontraditional" worker. They also worked to ensure there was greater access to apprenticeships and the trades, while also attempting to remove "glass ceilings" for those with the talents and desires to climb corporate ladders. The 1990s brought targeted enforcement, greater utilization of the media and its inherent multiplier effect, and a stronger rewards structure for those trying to do the right thing.

Though some may argue that their employer never bought into equal employment or diversity, the last decade brought philosophical changes to many workplaces. America's workplaces became more supportive of issues that affect workers, such as car pools, daycare, maternity/adoption leave, domestic partners and elder care. Seemingly overnight, employers began offering flexible maternity/paternity leave, daycare subsidies or actual daycare centers, on-site dry cleaning, lactation rooms and even dinners "on the run" at minimal costs.

While these policies seem to be worker-friendly, some critics are quick to point out that they are aimed at keeping the employee at work longer. Others argue that it is the employees' commitment that leads to these extra hours, and that these on-site amenities, fringe benefits or other elements of one's total rewards package are a way of showing corporate gratitude and commitment to a family-friendly environment. Whether cheered or jeered, America's employers have become aware of the trade-offs and competing demands that today's workers face.

Diversity as a Business Imperative

Many companies today have elevated diversity from a moral issue of the 1990s to a business strategy. This effort to groom diverse talent came about via a host of mechanisms. The initiatives undertaken in the spirit of diversity varied as greatly as the workplaces themselves. These included the use of:

- **Focus groups and exit surveys** in an attempt to identify specific issues and concerns of minority group members and women

- **Formal and informal diversity networks** that brought together minority group members and/or women from the corporate ranks. These groups often worked to change senior-level management's assumptions regarding particular workers and workplace issues.

- **Development of diversity bands** in which employees were clustered by title or position. Hiring and promotion goals were set according to the internal composition and external markets.

- **Outside consultants** as impartial observers to get the pulse of the work force and to isolate issues of concern.

- **Senior management's direct intervention in the demographics of the corporate pipeline.** In many of America's workplaces, senior managers began spending hours trying to ensure that, when cultivating future leaders, talented minority group members and women were not overlooked. These executives began asking the tough questions: "Why are there no minority group members on this slate?" "How far down into the ranks do we have to go to find a woman who might fill one of these management seats?"

- **Development of high-potential minority group member lists or lists of key female "promotables."** Many worked hard to ensure that talented people of color or women were not passed over for training opportunities and key exposures. These high-potential lists were used to ensure proper development and cross-fertilization. As a consequence, this would place minority group members and/or women in the succession plan for upper-level management positions.

A glance at just one diversity conference's program includes: "Measuring Diversity Results for Quantum Performance Impact," "Translating Soft Diversity Strategic Initiatives Into Hard Measurables," "Diversity Measurement: Moving from Initiatives to Bottom Line ROI," and "Building a Diversity Accountability Model: Linking Functional and Process Performance Measures to Create a Balanced Diversity Scorecard." While there is debate as to "what works best" in attracting, developing and retaining a diverse work force, it is clear that for many companies, fostering diversity is more than the right thing to do; it's a business goal.

In addition to formal diversity programs, corporate restructurings may have assisted in the advancement of many people of color and women. Companies realigning or merging often require formal job postings of their positions. Some workplaces require every job to be posted and each and every employee to apply and recompete for his/her current job or any other position they desire within the company. This required posting process assisted in corporate downsizing, as companies reduced their work forces using this system. This practice may have actually assisted in the advancement of talented minority group members and women, many of whom may have been overlooked when positions were networked rather than formally posted.

With regard to the impact of downsizing and restructuring, a research study filed with the Federal Glass Ceiling Commission found that white women, and to a lesser extent minority men, actually increased their representation in management both in absolute numbers and proportion to white men during a four-year period of downsizing.[2] Whatever the process embraced by employers during this time period, women and minority group members were becoming more visible throughout America's work force ranks.

Affirmative Action Backlash

The progress that minorities and women saw over the past decade has not been without costs. One of the biggest fallouts has been that gains in the workplace by minority group members or women sometimes are viewed as suspect. Examples of allegations or complaints may include: *"She only got the job because she's a woman,"* or *"I may as well not even apply for promotions anymore. They're all rigged for diversity."*

There often was mass confusion regarding the differences and nuances between affirmative action, equal employment opportunity and diversity. It should be noted that the entire concept of workplace equity is equality for all … not to benefit solely one group over another.

At times, cries of "reverse discrimination" were heard. How many reverse discrimination cases have been meritorious is difficult to answer. In his report, "The Social Construction of Reverse Discrimination: The Impact of Affirmative Action on Whites" (*Journal of Intergroup Relations*, Winter 2001/2002), Fred L. Pincus differentiates between reduced opportunities (due to the fact that there is a bigger pool of talent including people of color and women) and reverse discrimination. Pincus reports that studies vary from one-third of reverse discrimination suits having merit (Burstein 1991), to less than 1 percent (Reskin 1998). "These studies suggest that relatively few reverse discrimination court cases and EEOC complaints have legal merit," he said.[3]

Similarly, in a report by Alfred W. Blumrosen, a Rutgers University law professor, the U.S. District Courts and the Court of Appeals identified fewer than 100 reverse discrimination cases among more than 3,000 discrimination opinions over a four-year period. Of these, a high proportion lacked merit, while only six substantiated the claim and were granted relief.[4] Equal employment laws are no different from other employment laws, and need to be enforced fairly, across the board.

Some of the concern regarding reverse discrimination was due to the fact that workplace trends welcoming diversity and those downsizing were colliding. Companies struggled with how to realign their businesses to stay competitive without violating the EEO laws, affirmative action laws, the

Americans with Disabilities Act and the Age Discrimination in Employment Act of 1967 (ADEA). One example is the EEOC's $2.1 million settlement with Gulfstream Aerospace Corporation in December 2002 on behalf of employees 40 years of age or older who were laid off in violation of the ADEA during a reduction in force at the company's Savannah facility. The EEOC's district director stated:

"Reductions in force may be a necessary fact of economic life. However, employers cannot use downsizing as a means of eliminating older employees from their work force. Productive, hard-working employees with 20 to 30 years of experience deserve better than to be pushed out the door, while younger, less experienced individuals are retained."[5]

Where Is the Anticipated Diversity Today?

Workforce 2000 was published with much fanfare and publicity, yet it had a small typographical error in its narrative. That error, a single word omission, led to many of the dramatic changes in America's workplaces. While the report asserted that almost two-thirds of the new entrants to the work force between 1987 and 2000 would be women, and that 29 percent of the new entrants would be minority group members, the report ought to have stated net new entrants. While the corresponding tables were labeled properly, the omission in the narrative was an important distinction. The "net new entrants" represent the net gain after a white male replaces each white male. The inadvertent omission — though clarified in later press releases — never caught people's attention. Employers seemingly immediately began preparing for a markedly different work force than they had in 1987. Many of the worker-friendly workplace initiatives can be tied to this publication's predictions.

While the media emphasized the trend data forecasting this increased diversity, the *Workforce 2000* report also stated:

"The skill mix of the economy will be moving rapidly upscale, with most new jobs demanding more education and higher levels of language, math, and reasoning skill …."

This too went relatively underreported. "These occupational changes will present a difficult challenge for the disadvantaged, particularly for black men and Hispanics, who are underrepresented in the fastest growing professions and over-represented in the shrinking job categories."[6]

Those professions that projected an increase included: marketing and sales, technicians, teachers, managers, engineers, lawyers and natural scientists. Thus, the jobs of today and tomorrow will be more mentally demanding, and may be too great a hurdle for the disadvantaged.

So has there really been a dramatic change in America's work force? Carol D'Amico, co-author of *Workforce 2020: Work and Workers in the 21st Century*, the sequel to the Hudson Institute publication on workplace trends, said:

"In 1987 when *Workforce 2000* was published, it included predictions of radical changes in American business brought on by demographic changes. The fact is, we haven't really seen those radical changes yet. Basically, work looks a lot the same now as it did then."[7]

Much of the anticipated demographic change has not occurred. Yet, we have seen much advancement for women and people of color. How are those talented minority group members and women who are working in America's work force faring today? Have we rooted out bias and discrimination in hiring and promotion?

The Persistence of Access Problems

It is clear that access problems still exist. There are entire occupations with a dearth of minority group members or women … sometimes due to lack of requisite skills, other times by choice, and yet still other times by exclusion.

Certainly, educational attainment and skill development will help ensure that tomorrow's workers have the tools they need to compete. If the jobs of tomorrow demand higher levels of language, math and reasoning, ensuring our schools meet this demand is vital. Minority group members and women are underrepresented in many high-tech professions today and this will not soon be remedied due to their relative absence in the requisite college and university pipeline.

What about those who have the skills, talent and desire to work hard and contribute? Is there fairness in hiring and promotional processes throughout America's workplaces? How can we be sure that qualified minorities and women are considered for employment and/or promotion when we ourselves know that many jobs are filled by word-of-mouth and networking? How are the mid- and upper-level jobs in your workplace filled? How many lunches or casual conversations does it take before a person should be considered an applicant for employment? Though there have been many success stories of minorities and women who have "made it," our focus should remain steadfast to ensure that all jobs are open to those with the relevant qualifications (excluding of course those jobs in which gender is a bona fide occupational qualification, for example, female bathroom attendants in women's restrooms).

During the '90s the federal government became quite adept in this pursuit and in using the press to get the message out. Headlines would blare: "Forty-Nine Women Kept Out of Blue Collar Positions to Share Discrimination Settlement."

Yet, despite the media's attention, for some the problem of getting one's foot in the door still prevails, from a bank in the South that was fined $225,000 for disproportionately hiring Caucasians over 132 qualified minority group members in entry-level clerical positions to more than $1 million awarded to black and Hispanic job applicants discriminated against in hiring at a Las Vegas Hotel.

For those who do get in the door, promotional and career track discrimination remains a challenge — from entry-level management positions in nontraditional fields to global assignments and partnerships in law and accounting firms. Some will profess that it's "just a matter of time" before these groups are promoted. Others will state that minority group members or women will not and should not be promoted due to a lack of educational attainment; that discrimination has become more subtle and hard to specifically identify; that it is outright, unlawful, blatant discrimination. Regardless of the reasons, placement issues, often referred to as access discrimination,[8] are evident.

Each year millions of dollars are collected from companies having failed (or refusing) to promote members of protected groups within their work force. In 2001, the EEOC reached a $2.2 million settlement on behalf of one female employee who actually developed and trained a newly hired male employee. After doing so, the establishment transferred almost all of her job functions to him, leading her to complain. This led ultimately to her termination ... while paying him more to do her job. "The $2.2 million verdict sends a strong message ... that loyalty to the 'Old Boys Club' cannot serve to justify employment decisions which favor males at the expense of female employees," stated the EEOC Regional Attorney.[9]

While hiring and placement patterns and promotional opportunities are important concerns, they have become relatively routine matters for many employers and for federal and state investigators. Ensuring that all are being paid fairly no matter what level they hold in America's work force is an even greater challenge and a growing concern.

Paycheck Equity

Access discrimination, while not eradicated, has at least been tempered. *Valuation discrimination*, based on the pay that women and minorities receive for the jobs they perform, continues. Such pay inequities may be exacerbated in nontraditional fields. A poll by Financial Women International, an organization of 13,000 women in executive financial positions, found that 98 percent *believe* that women are paid less than white males with the same skills, education and experience in the same or comparable position within their industry. An astounding 83 percent felt they had personally suffered from unequal pay in the same job as a white man. The American Bar Association Committee on Status of Women in the profession found that female attorneys with similar backgrounds and one year of experience typically begin earning $1,000 less than men, by mid-career, women with four to nine years of experience earn $8,000 less, and by 10 to 20 years, they earn $22,000 less.[10]

Earnings data from the U.S. Department of Labor's Bureau of Labor Statistics demonstrate that there continues to be a vast pay differential between male and female wages. While that gap has narrowed during the last decade or more, full-time women workers today earn only 73 percent as much as full-time male workers.[11] While this is up from 62.5 percent in 1979, this still is incredibly low for a nation that prides itself on fairness. Couple this with the fact that men's real earnings have actually fallen since 1973, and that wage advancement is less credible. "No matter how it has been measured, we find that women's earnings continue to be below those received by men. In essentially all occupations for which information is available, women's median weekly earnings are less than men's earnings."[12]

At the highest levels of corporate America, even though the number of minority group members or women incumbents is small, the pay disparity is even greater. Debra Meyerson, a visiting professor at Stanford University who studies gender issues, states: "The more senior they get, the more subtle the barriers become, and the more profoundly they operate." Nowhere is inequity at the top more apparent than in pay.[13]

In September 2001, the EEOC filed a lawsuit against Morgan Stanley Dean Witter & Co. on behalf of a female former convertible bond sales representative and 100 other women who the EEOC claims were being compensated less than their male colleagues. It appears that Ms. Allison Schieffelin, a former convertible bond sales representative, and many other women in Morgan Stanley's Institutional Equity Division allege they were not only compensated less than their male colleagues, but had their professional advancement limited as well. Ms. Schieffelin was ultimately fired.

According to Spencer H. Lewis, Jr., director of the EEOC's New York district office charged with handling this matter, "Morgan Stanley systematically denied opportunities for equal compensation and advancement to a class of professional women. By filing this pattern or practice case the EEOC seeks to remedy these illegal practices and send a message that discrimination will not be tolerated in this or any other industry."

Equal pay is of enormous concern to women ... perhaps the highest for many. During the 1990s, the Women's Bureau of the U.S. Department of Labor conducted a major national survey to ask working women about their jobs. More than a quarter-million women responded. "Improving pay scales" was their top priority for change.[14] Similarly, for unionized workers, the AFL-CIO reports: "Hands down the top concern for women workers is equal pay."[15]

Whose Responsibility Is It?

One of the eye-opening findings of the U.S. Department of Labor's reports on "glass ceilings" released in the early 1990s was the fact that generally, in most companies audited by the DOL, no individual was working to ensure nondiscrimination in compensation. While elaborate compensation systems are developed, modified and implemented at major U.S. employers, ensuring that they are working equitably has not been seen as a priority.

> **Definition**
>
> **Glass ceilings** coined in the 1980s, refer to subtle barriers that prevent qualified minority group members and women from attaining the mid- and upper-levels of America's workplaces. Minority group members and women can see these upper levels, but cannot attain them. This initiative raised management's awareness to placement patterns — staff positions vs. line positions. For example, those who were qualified for and interested in line jobs often were steered into staff jobs. Promotional issues became apparent as well.

While many individuals play a role in this arena, who is in the best position to effect change immediately? The compensation professional develops, designs and implements balanced, innovative and flexible systems to reward employees. The equal employment officer is knowledgeable of the legal nondiscrimination requirements that all HR systems must meet. The HR generalist is integral in the day-to-day management of all HR responsibilities.

Who among these should spearhead this effort? At whose feet should this responsibility rest? The balance of this book is dedicated to illuminating these issues and recommending solutions.

2

Studies and Secrecy

*A*t a recent dinner party I was asked what I was "up to these days." Not knowing when I'd finish writing this book and not wanting everyone I knew to ask, I just briefly mumbled something about doing some writing on equal pay. After a brief discussion, a man I knew socially looked at me as if he'd seen a ghost. He blurted out, "You mean I can't pay the men who work for me whatever I want, even if it means I pay them more than the women?" There was a moment of silence as I assessed how to best respond in this setting but before I could answer, his wife informed him that he was correct and that to do so, without just cause, would be illegal. She then informed him how she had personally seen pay equity issues affect her industry over the years. He became enlightened that evening.

The wage gap between men and women and minority group members and Caucasians is what's called a "hot button issue." It is not the type of issue one would want to bring up at a cocktail party, as it is one in which almost everyone seems to have an opinion and a personal vignette.

While many still just don't get it, their understanding of and interest in the issue increases exponentially when it affects their spouse or children. Robert Reich, former secretary of the U.S. Department of Labor, wrote in an article for *The Boston Globe* that the day he became a feminist was the day his wife was denied tenure at Harvard University.

In that article, Reich writes, "[A] string of white males had been voted tenure just before her. Most had not written as much as she, nor inspired the same praise from specialists around the nation as her work. None of their writings had been subjected to the detailed scrutiny — footnote by footnote — to which her colleagues had subjected her latest manuscript ...."16

Things somehow become very clear when we know the people involved. That is not to say that all wage differences are due to bias or discrimination. There are a number of reasons that the wage gap exists between men and women. Just ask someone. They will certainly have an opinion.

Differences of Opinion on Pay Inequity

- It's just a matter of time before the wage gap narrows completely.
- Differences are accounted for by the industry and occupations that men and women choose.
- Men and women differ in their average work hours, with women leaving early to get home to their families.
- If you take education and experience into account, there is very little difference.
- Women take time off to have children, and that's the reason there's a pay differential.
- It's due to the fact that when women begin to fill any job in large numbers, there is a correlating decline in value of that position and a decline in pay.
- The women in those fields are younger and less senior.
- It's discrimination — plain, old-fashioned race and gender discrimination.

There also is the view that it is a bad thing for women to receive equity pay increases. Those who support this view have asserted that enforcement of equal pay laws would benefit some job incumbents while actually reducing the overall employment opportunities of men and women. These individuals advocate that while some women or people of color may be underpaid, it's better to just leave things as they are.

Surveys and studies abound by state and industry. Very little time passes before yet another study or survey is released supporting either side of the issue. This public policy organization states the gap is growing; that one says it's shrinking. This longitudinal study states the gap is closing; that one says the gap is only occupation-specific. This study is of hourly workers; that one is of managers. Even the federal government weighs in. The General Accounting Office reported in 2002 that "female managers are not only making less money than men in many industries, but the wage gap has also deepened during the economic boom years of 1995 to 2000."[17]

Yet, for each study that cites occupation or work hours as the root of wage differentials, there is an opposing finding. For example, while many argue the wage disparity is occupation-specific, the National Bureau of Economic Research found that while this does account for a large part of the disparity, "a substantial part of this gap remains attributable to the individual's sex .... [O]ur results leave open the possibility that within narrowly-defined occupations and establishments, men and women are performing essentially the same job but are not being paid equally — a violation of the Equal Pay Act."[18]

So, what's the truth? What's significant to us today? Does general salary information and historical data dampen our responsibilities to compensate our workers fairly? Everyone has an anecdote and opinion. If our worldview is one of bias and discrimination, it could be based upon personal injustices affecting our loved ones or ourselves. Conversely, if our worldview is one of equity, we may believe those who cry racism or sexism hold improper career assumptions or compensation assertions. While everyone has a vignette or a study to which they can refer, our views vary widely. The best sources of information regarding compensation are those with access to actual employment data. That world is very limited. Those in "the know" include employers, certain managers and attorneys, compensation professional(s) and those who audit and investigate employers to ensure non-discrimination.

Why not ask employees themselves? Isn't wage information generally public information? While this generally is true for state and federal government workers, this is not the case for many of America's workers.

If differentiation is not a bad thing and it is based upon performance or other employee-specific aspects vital to the employer (e.g., sales, performance goals, etc.), why is there such secrecy? Why don't employees know how they fare with their peers? Not only is such information not readily available to the average employee, in many cases, they are told they may not discuss their salary with others. In some cases they may even sign a confidentiality agreement such as:

In consideration of my employment by the Corporation and of the further continuation of such employment, and of the salary or wages paid to me in connection with such employment and for other good and valuable consideration, I agree as follows: not to divulge such confidential information as … salary and other forms of compensation …

It is this secrecy that fosters concerns. While often it is for proprietary reasons and to prevent corporate raiding, it also could be to ensure that workers are not able to readily make salary comparisons. In the EEOC vs. Morgan Stanley Dean Witter & Co. suit mentioned earlier, the U.S. magistrate Ronald L. Ellis ruled that Morgan Stanley must share salary data with the litigants for this very reason. "Because compensation and promotion data is such a closely guarded secret, many women may not know definitively if they were victims of discrimination."[19]

Why are studies of wages so conflicting? Why isn't salary information available? Why do lawyers and managers go to great lengths to label such information confidential? Why do companies being audited by the federal government go to great lengths to keep this information from investigators? Why the lack of open communication when most HR practitioners would argue that good communication is vital to the effectiveness of HR systems and practices? If there are no salary concerns, why the secrecy? These are important questions.

3

The Law and
One's Compensation

"Some say that market forces will take care of the wage gap. If we had relied on market forces, we would have never passed the Civil Rights Act, the Family and Medical Leave Act or the Americans with Disabilities Act."

— *U.S. Senator Tom Harkin (D-IA)*

T he search for economic equity has a long history in U.S. labor law. While there are several laws and implementing regulations regarding compensation on record today, their origin goes back to the early 1940s.

"As early as World War II, the National War Labor Board was created as the arbiter of salary disputes between labor and management. In 1942, it issued an order for salary adjustments to 'equalize the wage or salary rates paid to females with rates paid to males for comparable quality and quantity of work on the same or similar operations.' A bill requiring 'equal pay for comparable work' performed by males and females was introduced in Congress in 1945 and rejected, as were several similar bills, over the next 18 years."[20]

Since that time, The Equal Pay Act of 1963, Title VII of the Civil Rights Act of 1964, the Age Discrimination in Employment Act of 1967 and Executive Order 11246 all have attempted to address these issues.

The Equal Pay Act prohibits dissimilar pay for equal or substantially equal work performed by men and women. "Substantially equal" has been interpreted to mean that the jobs are performed in the same working establishment, equal in skill, effort and responsibility, and must be performed under similar working conditions.

The four factors used to determine if the work is substantially the same are:

1. **Skill:** Experience, training, education and ability, as measured by the performance requirements of a particular job.

2. **Effort:** Mental or physical. The amount or degree of effort (not type of effort) actually expended in the performance of a job.

3. **Responsibility:** The degree of accountability required in the performance of a job.

4. **Working Conditions:** The physical surroundings and hazards of a job including dimensions such as inside versus outside work, heat/cold or poor ventilation.

There are lawful justifications for pay differentials, including seniority, merit and shift differentials, to name a few.

Title VII of the Civil Rights Act of 1964 prohibits discrimination on the basis of race, sex, color, national origin or religion in all employment practices. Practices covered by this act include hiring, firing, promotion and compensation.

Since 1964, the courts have clarified that such discrimination can be proven under either the theory of disparate treatment or the theory of disparate impact.

Executive Order 11246 is a presidential directive that applies the protections of Title VII of the Civil Rights Act to all companies that do business with the federal government. This includes most major businesses, banks and other corporate entities.

> Two theories of discrimination exist under Title VII. Disparate treatment refers to unequal or different (other than favorable) treatment of minority group members or women in the workplace (eg., harsher performance standards for the latter group). Disparate impact refers to personnel practices which may have a differential, adverse impact upon protected groups regardless of intent.

On the face of it, with all of these federal laws (and many state and community fair employment laws), one would think compensation discrimination would have been rooted out long ago. While these statutes exist, investigating and proving compensation discrimination remains a difficult task. While it may be difficult to ensure pay equity, it is not impossible.

How large is the pay gap between minority group members and Caucasians? Between men and women? As discussed previously, these are areas of great dispute. There is general consensus that the wage gap between men and women is roughly 25 to 27 cents on the dollar, and is greater between minority group members and Caucasians. What determines or affects this gap is often contested and depends on one's point of view.

Oversight Committees and Public Interest Groups

Oversight agencies, such as the U.S. Civil Rights Commission, have oft noted this pay disparity. The National Committee on Pay Equity (NCPE), founded in 1979, has been working to end this differential for more than two decades. Numerous state and local organizations are committed to this issue, such as the National Commission on Working Women,

> The NCPE is a national coalition of labor and women's civil rights organizations which work together toward the mutual goal of elimination of sex- and race-based wage discrimination and the achievement of pay equity.

Wider Opportunities for Women, the NETWORK: A Catholic Social Justice Lobby, large labor unions and the Older Women's League. The cry for pay equity covers almost every industry and level of income.

Though these organizations, commissions and oversight committees do not have law enforcement authority, federal and state agencies not only administer these equal pay laws, but can fine offenders and even prevent them from obtaining contracts with the U.S. government.

The "Cops on the Beat"

While there are not enough federal investigators for some, there are too many for others. Some compensation settlements with these federal forces have brought banner headlines:

- *"Boeing Agrees to End Pay Disparity. Second Largest Federal Contractor Will Adjust Pay Practices Corporate Wide"* [11/19/99]

- *"Texaco to Pay $3.1 M to Women Professionals and Executives in Largest Pay Discrimination Settlement"* [1/6/99]

- *"R.R. Donnelly Agrees to $425,000 Settlement to Resolve Wage Disparities Within Its Professional and Management Staff"* [9/30/98]

- *"American Greetings Corporation Agrees to $217,000 Compensation Case Settlement with U.S. Department of Labor"* [10/7/97]

The Equal Employment Opportunity Commission

While there are auditors and investigators at state and local enforcement agencies, it is the federal government that has the greatest nationwide oversight and enforcement. The Equal Employment Opportunity Commission (EEOC) is headquartered in Washington, D.C., with regional and satellite offices throughout the United States. While the Wage and Hour Division of the U.S. Department of Labor originally enforced the Equal Pay

Act, enacted in 1963, it has been part of the EEOC's enforcement arsenal since 1979. The EEOC has no "proactive" Equal Pay Act enforcement unless it establishes a commissioner's charge on behalf of a "class of individuals." Instead, the EEOC's equal pay caseload is based upon individual charges and complaints and enforced through Title VII and/or the Equal Pay Act.

If an employee believes he or she has been denied a job; paid less; passed over for a promotion; or discriminated against in some other way, he or she can file a complaint with the local EEOC office. Such filings must be within 180 days of the discriminatory action. The local EEOC office even will help prepare the employees' case and advise them of their legal rights. If the EEOC believes the case has merit, it will investigate. The following is an example of the EEOC's enforcement in the area of pay equity:

McKesson Water Products Company and Groupe Danone, Calif. $1.2 million on behalf of a class of minority group members who charged that McKesson paid African-American drivers less and increased their compensation at a slower rate than white drivers (among other issues).

Equal pay is just one of the EEOC's mandates. Others include enforcement of prohibitions against race discrimination, sex/gender discrimination, age discrimination, retaliation, discrimination based upon disabilities, discrimination based upon religion and discrimination based upon national origin.

U.S. Department of Labor's Office of Federal Contract Compliance Programs

The Office of Federal Contract Compliance Programs (OFCCP) is a branch of the Employment Standards Administration of the U.S. Department of Labor. The OFCCP has a nationwide network of regional and district offices in major metropolitan centers. While the agency administers several laws, this section will address Title VII of the Civil Rights Act of 1964 and Executive Order 11246.

Title VII of the Civil Rights Act of 1964 prohibits discrimination in hiring or employment opportunities on the basis of race, color, sex, religion and national origin. Executive Order 11246 prohibits employment discrimination and requires affirmative efforts by all contractors and subcontractors holding federal contracts which aggregate to $10,000 or more in any one year, and any contractor that has a single federal contract or subcontract of $50,000 or more and a corporatewide work force of 50 or more people. In short, its reach extends to most large U.S. employers. The agency also has several "memoranda of understanding" with the EEOC ensuring joint enforcement and coordination. As a manager, you should know whether your entity falls under the auspices of the OFCCP and the responsibilities and legal requirements of such.

The OFCCP enforces its mandates through compliance reviews and complaint investigations. It is these proactive compliance reviews that give the U.S. government its strongest oversight in the area of nondiscrimination and equal pay. While the EEOC has equal pay enforcement responsibilities, its workload is primarily complaint-driven. The OFCCP proactively audits most major U.S. businesses to ensure nondiscrimination. In addition, because of its access to a wide variety of compensation data, the OFCCP focuses more on systemic, or pattern and practice, discrimination affecting large numbers of people.

Some landmark cases in pay discrimination brought in by the OFCCP include:

- CoreStates Financial Institution, headquartered in Philadelphia. In that settlement, CoreStates "will address past practices of pay discrimination against women and minority bank employees." The agreement called for $1,150,434 in back pay. Additionally, salary adjustments would be awarded to 76 women and 66 minorities to the tune of $334,115. (1998)

- Blue Cross Blue Shield of Maryland. $500,000 in back pay and salary increases to 57 women who held "equal or higher qualifications than men in the same career band [and] were compensated at the known market value for their jobs, but men were compensated above the known market value for their jobs." (1996)

While women are making strides in obtaining positions in management and even the executive ranks, their pay still lags.

- U.S. Airways Corp. of Arlington, Va. The OFCCP revealed a pay discrepancy between men and women in the executive levels of the company. U.S. Airways agreed to pay $306,066 in back pay to 30 women and an additional $83,984 in base salary adjustments to 26 of the women. (1998)

Ensuring nondiscrimination in compensation is just one of the many laws that both the EEOC and the OFCCP enforce. There are investigators in America's workplaces, but are they up to the task? With limited experience in compensation systems development and implementation, federal investigators have a daunting task. Thus, the federal government has adopted some broad-brush measures to review pay to ensure equity. The approach has a rudimentary component and a more formal regression analysis, and reflects the mandate to ensure equity in the workplace.

Requirement of an Annual Submission

Currently, the compensation professional may not be actively involved in the world of equal employment opportunity, especially if there is not an active audit occurring at one's workplace. While the OFCCP also is conducting a pilot project that requires an annual submission of salary data for an EO survey of companies that fall within its purview, the EEO officer may download such from an HR information system without any consultation with the compensation professional. Employers and counsel have a host of worries about the confidentiality of such submissions. One of their greatest concerns is how the federal government analyzes the data, and whether it will be used inappropriately to target employers for audits.

Rather than submissions of raw data, another approach would be to require companies to perform their own analysis for submission to the federal government. In their book, *Legalizing Gender Inequality*, Robert L. Nelson and William P. Bridges note that the Canadian province of Ontario requires such pay studies and grants a form of "limited immunity" from discrimination lawsuits for companies that undertake the recommendations of the pay study.[21] They argue that if such was required of the largest U.S. employers, the "results might be quite dramatic." This form of self-auditing has merit. But why limit it to only those companies that hold contracts with the federal government and fall within the OFCCP's purview? Why exempt the small employer where much of the current job growth has been occurring? An audit of a very small employer would not be laborious or time-consuming. Short of this requirement and submission, it is up to each of us to proactively ensure fairness within our own work forces.

Privatization of Pay Equity?

Due to the limited number of investigators and their relative lack of compensation experience, some federal offices are moving toward hiring or subcontracting compensation analyses to statisticians and/or mathematicians. Rather than filling this void on a regional or "spotty basis," some advocate moving this function to the private sector. The federal government could contract out this responsibility in entirety to businesses whose employees are skilled in

EEO, compensation and mathematical modeling. While there would have to be safeguards and assurances made to protect the confidentiality of the data, the notion of privatizing the federal government's nondiscrimination mandates to the private sector is not without backing and merit.

U.S. Congress Weighing In

Because of the heightened awareness of pay discrimination, the 106th and 107th Congress brought forth several bills for consideration that contend directly with this issue. The Fair Pay Act of 1999 (S.684/H.R. 1362) addressed these issues from a societal point of view. Among other items, the act held that within individual companies, an employer could not make the salaries of jobs held predominantly by women less than those held by men if the jobs are equivalent in value to the employer. While this was interpreted by many as a vehicle for comparable worth, it also may have codified the current process used by the U.S. Department of Labor's OFCCP. There has been no action on this bill.

By contrast, the Paycheck Fairness Act (S.77/H.R. 781) introduced during the 107th Congress sought to strengthen the Equal Pay Act of 1963. In addition to setting wage levels and increased penalties and damages for violators, the act required the OFCCP to "provide training to Commission employees and affected individuals and entities on matters involving discrimination in the payment of wages." If these pieces of legislation were enacted, who should conduct the training and what that training should consist of are important issues warranting further discussion.

4

Identifying Salary Discrimination

"When our institution published the results of an internal pay study, I went to my department chair and said, 'How can this be? How can I, a director of a research center and full professor, fall in the bottom quartile of the salary range? You are hiring new Ph.D.s and paying them more!' After some vague assertions, I queried, 'Do you think that would hold up in court?' Needless to say, I got a raise."

— *Female University Professor*

What is salary discrimination? Do you think you know it when you see it? How can you be sure? As employees, wouldn't it be nice to *know* that you are being paid properly? Wouldn't it be comforting to *know* your employer conducts internal equity reviews to ensure nondiscrimination? As managers, shouldn't we be ensuring that salary concerns do not arise at all, or warrant a remedy when they do occur? Wouldn't it benefit us to be able to assert that as a baseline, we conduct internal audits to help ensure fairness in all forms of compensation?

For the compensation professional who designs and administers various compensation programs, wouldn't it be comforting to know these programs are being implemented equitably? How many times have managers tweaked the system or asked for just one more deviation from policy? Too many "exceptions to the rule" or one-offs can invalidate any system and cause further frustration.

Determining what salary discrimination is — and is not — has been a major preoccupation for employers and law enforcers for many years. Because a wide variety of factors can affect pay, how should it be properly analyzed?

Who is/are the best person(s) to conduct such analyses? Who should review your compensation systems in your work force?

While state regulatory agencies oversee non-discrimination in America's workplaces, the federal government has the greatest external oversight in this area. Is it the best suited for this feat? Should the HR manager help or hinder such an outside review? What role, if any, does a compensation professional play during an investigation by the federal government? How does the federal government conduct its analyses? This chapter will focus on the many methodologies used to audit base pay and make recommendations as how to do so properly.

The U.S. Department of Labor's Women's Bureau, an educational and advocacy branch of the DOL, offers the following guidelines to keep your company within compliance.

10 Steps to an Equal Pay Self-Audit for Employers

1. Conduct a recruitment self-audit.

2. Evaluate your compensation system for internal equity.

3. Evaluate your compensation system for industry competitiveness.

4. Conduct a new job evaluation system if needed.

5. Examine your compensation system and compare job grades/scores.

6. Review data for personnel entering your company.

7. Assess opportunity for employees to win commissions and bonuses.

8. Assess how raises are awarded.

9. Evaluate employee training, development and promotion opportunities.

10. Implement changes where needed, maintain equity and share your successes.

The following sections will cover all of the compensation-related issues concerning these guidelines.

Initial Placement

The issue of initial job placement is critical from the onset. Specific job placement is vital to one's career path and one's remuneration. At many companies assignment to a certain business route, product line and business unit can make or break one's career and has a direct tie to one's compensation package. While this may not be the starting point for an audit by an outside federal investigative body, such reviews often circle back to this component when salary skews or large differentials are identified. Thus, the initial placement should be a vital aspect of a thorough proactive internal review. While this may lie outside the compensation professional's direct realm of responsibilities, it is advised that the HR officers, the personnel staff, and the recruitment and hiring professional be knowledgeable of the EEO ramifications of initial job placements. Do these professionals work to ensure nondiscrimination in such decisions? Are such placement decisions proactively monitored in the work force to ensure equal access?

Example: LetUsHelp Company just hired three new corporate counsels right out of law school. The only female has been assigned the corporate cases involving personnel practices and human resources, while the two males have been offered the occupational safety and health issues and matters concerning labor-management relations. Why are the males given the labor-management/union issues within LetUsHelp Company? Is this by preference? Is it based upon prior work experience or clerk positions? Is there a presumption that men are better negotiators? Which caseload will make a greater impact on the company? Will some areas and cases/clients be more lucrative financially and a more direct route to general counsel? Is anyone within human resources looking at these issues for "steering" and fairness? These initial job placements most likely will dictate future earnings potential and career growth for all three.

Once in a career path, business unit or product line, it often is difficult to transfer, move laterally or be promoted out. In addition to the legal field, these workload issues are important in many other professions. In sales, marketing and finance, for example, there often are more direct routes that can lead to higher salaries and rewards and a quicker path to the top. Mid- and entry-level management is not always aware of these placement and steering concerns. This can be seen anecdotally in the 1995 *Minority Retention Survey* conducted by Brecker & Merryman Inc., where minority group members felt that "regardless of official policies and sincere interest in diversity at senior management levels, many respondents said that middle managers and immediate supervisors often thwart the career prospects of minorities.[22]

This issue has arisen time and again during audits of corporate salaries on a broad scale. When an overall systemic review indicates unusually low salaries for minority group members or women, a closer look may isolate the pattern within certain business units or functions. The lower salaries may be due to certain functions or business lines having larger budgets or being better performing. The corporate rationale often dictates that these units have had a greater impact on the bottom line, and therefore receive a larger pool of money for performance awards. Such audits can quickly turn to one of demographics, diversity and discrimination. Why is it that the minority group members and/or women are in the unit that either does not or cannot affect the bottom line as well or as readily? Are these individuals clustered into these units by choice? By chance? By steering? All such workload decisions and assignments should be routinely monitored to ensure equal access, as they help ensure there is equal footing for all.

Starting Salary

One's starting salary often determines future pay progression, as well. While the compensation division may set the salary target or range for new hires, the setting of specific wages generally falls outside the compensation profes- sional's duties and responsibilities. While the HR generalist or hiring manager may call upon the compensation professional to grant an exception to the starting salary range or target, starting salaries, more than likely, are not questioned. While compensation professionals are in a prime position to question any or all who are outside the salary ranges of the system, they may not be consulted at all.

To ensure the integrity of a system, guidance should be promulgated, clearly articulating starting salary ranges and the objective standards for variations. Such guidance should be clear and concise, and provide specifics regarding the experiences and exposures that may lead to starting salary differentials. In addition to reviewing below/above salary range decisions, the compensation professional should bring any starting salary concerns or patterns that arise to senior management's attention. It bears repeating that the more "exceptions to the rule" that are allowed to exist within the compensation system, the less one can claim a system actually exists. A partnership between the compensation professional, the hiring manager and the human resource generalist will assist in ensuring there is nondiscrimi- nation in salary offers and starting salaries.

The goal of fairness or pay equity can begin and end at starting salaries. Differentials in starting salaries become institutionalized, with merit increases generally a percentage of base pay. If two new hires have a substantial salary differential at the start, the lower-paid employee will never "catch up" regardless of exceptional performance. While it would be an oversight not to mention the fact that the individual plays a key role in negotiating salary, the hiring manager should not only be knowledgeable of the need to ensure equity at time of hire, but should ensure that any deviations or "exceptions to the rule" can be justified and documented.

> "Often when we find a situation where the men are paid more than the women in entry-level positions, we are told by the company that the men negotiated for a higher starting salary. This sets in motion a differential that is generally never overcome."
>
> — *Federal Investigator*

FIGURE 1: PAYMENOW COMPANY				
Title	**Race/ Gender**	**Starting Salary**	**Performance Rating**	**Merit Increase**
Systems Administrator I	Caucasian/ Male	$32,500	2	3%
Systems Administrator I	Black/Male	$28,500	1	2%
Systems Administrator I	Caucasian/Female	$29,500	2	2%

Note: The example is at the start of three individuals' careers. Imagine the variations that can occur over time if not reviewed.

In Figure 1, all three employees were new hires last year. The manager who determined starting salary, annual performance ratings and merit increases would most likely never have been questioned on his or her decisions, assuming each starting salary fell within the salary guidelines and end-of-the-year merit increases were below threshold. Yet, if the company encouraged proactive reviews, this manager might be queried as to:

- **Starting Salaries:** All three were new hires last year; why the starting salary differentials? Can the $4,000 differential between lowest and highest paid be justified? Are the reasons documented?

- **Ratings:** Does the written documentation (i.e., performance appraisal, etc.) correlate with the ratings given?

- **Percentage Merit Increase:** Why did the Caucasian male with a performance rating of "2" (on a scale of 1-5 with 1 the "best") receive a greater percentage merit increase than the others, particularly the black male with the higher performance rating?

There may be a lawful reason to explain some of these differentials. Prior work experience, advanced educational degrees and prior salary may lead to starting salary differentials, or when reviewed on a comparative basis, subtle biases may emerge. Educating the hiring manager to these issues, coupled with a proactive review on a routine basis, will ensure equity and assist in remedying unjustified salary differences before they become large dollar differentials with costly litigation. It is vital to remember that a lower starting salary at the start of one's career may prove impossible to overcome.

This type of title-by-title analysis was the basic salary analysis until the early 1990s. Until that point, the EEOC and the OFCCP had for the most part used this "exact same title" approach for salary analyses. First-year lawyers might form a "class" for comparative purposes. Similarly, a tool and dye operator would be compared with other tool and dye operators; a senior secretary level IV would be compared with other level IV senior secretaries, etc.

In instances where salary differentials are extremely large, an employer would have to justify such variations. Assuming the jobs are grouped properly for comparison, valid reasons can explain some salary variations and might include:

- New to job
- On-call pay
- Longer time in grade
- A seniority system
- Performance differences.

All of these are legitimate reasons for pay differentials. Upon examination, however, pay differentials may be unexplainable. In these instances salary remedies are required.

One evening a woman whom I know socially came to my home accompanied by her husband. She asked if she could come inside and chat with me … professionally. It appears that "Jane" had been given a raise: an out-of-cycle raise. In giving her such, her manager stated: "This is an affirmative action bump." Jane's husband did not feel comfortable with her accepting it. She felt almost guilty in taking it as she *didn't feel it was earned. After much discussion, I assured her that there was **no** such thing as an affirmative action pay increase. Rather, someone may have either performed an internal compensation audit, or an investigative body might have conducted such, and found her to be underpaid. She felt better at the end of our discussion, and while she wondered how many years this may have occurred, she did not want to pursue the issue of retroactive back pay.*

In this scenario, Jane's salary may have been found to be low when compared with others on a title-by-title basis. Or, a systemic review by an entire salary grade may have been performed. In either case, it appears Jane's salary was identified for a pay increase. I found it interesting that the manager referred to the salary increase as an "affirmative action raise." Was this ignorance? Was the manager aware of the difference between affirmative action and salary discrimination? Was it intentional to make Jane feel as if the money was not earned? The important point is that employers should conduct the analyses and be prepared to make salary adjustments where necessary.

Same Title — Two Salary Grades

It is important to note that special attention should be paid to job titles that encumber two salary grades. Is it the exact same job title utilizing two salary grades? If so, is it for career progression? Are there different standards at time of initial placement? Are there skills that differentiate the two? Are there lawful reasons for these salary grade differences? Are the requirements documented? Care must be taken to ensure that such differentiation is clearly identified and that there are no person-specific practices. If this type of system is utilized, job titles that cover two salary grades should have job descriptions that are markedly different and routinely audited to ensure nonbiased placement decisions.

The Baseline: A Cohort Job-by-Job Analysis

A salary review by job title (or those holding the same job description) is one of the most long-standing approaches to ensuring nondiscrimination. It is exactly that — a review of the wages of individuals holding the same title. The analysis centers on comparing jobs that have the same title and require the same skill and effort, responsibility and working conditions. To conduct this audit properly, one first should group employees holding the same job into legitimate sub-groupings or categories. These subgroupings are an important first step as they may assist in explaining pay differentials. Such subgroups might include:

- Part-time vs. full-time positions
- Shift work (to account for shift differentials)
- Training programs (perhaps providing a training wage)
- Working retiree programs
- Contract employees.

In very small work forces, this review on a person-by-person, job-by-job basis would suffice. This might be the case at more than four million U.S. firms with fewer than 50 employees.[23]

After grouping by title, one should ensure that any differentiation in pay or other forms of remuneration are justifiable and work-related. To do so, individual managers might have to justify pay decisions or salary increases on a person-by-person basis. Initial salary and specific job functions also should be reviewed to ensure nondiscrimination. A discussion of lawful reasons for pay differentiation is discussed later in this chapter.

In large work forces with multitudes of individuals holding the exact same title, after grouping into legitimate subgroups, a listing of salaries from highest to lowest within title is warranted. This title-by-title compensation matrix, a racking and stacking, should include the employee identifier, race, gender, time in job/job title, time in grade, performance rating, years of service, salary and salary increase, if available, in a database format. In an ideal world, the matrix also would include "recommended increases" and "recommended bonuses," as well as any other compensation variables that may be available for review prior to issuance. This will allow oversight and approval before implementation.

When reviewing these for comparative purposes, look for obvious aberrations such as a "superior" rated female or minority group member with a markedly low increase, or a minority group member with a high rating, many years of service and low salary increase or low pay. Such a matrix is important for annual review. Whether created by the EEO officer, downloaded by the HR professional or provided from a program developed by the compensation division, such a matrix is beneficial to ensure that any gross aberrations in base pay can be explained. A full review of personnel files should be conducted when salaries are in question.

Figure 2 is an example of the title-by-title approach. This represents a matrix of pay patterning for market analysts in salary grade 14. It appears that market analysts can hold this job function while in salary grade 13 as well, thus the time in job, time in grade differential. It appears that there may have been some direct hiring from outside the company into this salary grade over the past year.

Identifier	Race	Gender	Time/Job	Seniority	Time in Grade	Perf. Rate	Salary
A	W	M	4.5 yrs.	9.5 yrs.	2.7 yrs.	2	$62,000
B	W	M	3.9 yrs.	8.5 yrs.	2.8 yrs.	3	$61,000
C	W	M	2.9 yrs.	7.9 yrs.	2.5 yrs.	1	$61,000
D	A/PI	M	4.5 yrs.	8 yrs.	2.8 yrs.	2	$59,000
E	W	F	3.9 yrs.	7.5 yrs.	2.8 yrs.	2	$58,350
F	W	F	5.0 yrs.	10 yrs.	3.0 yrs.	2	$57,000
G	W	M	4.0 yrs.	7.4 yrs.	2.7 yrs.	3	$56,500
H	H	M	2.0 yrs.	6.5 yrs.	2.0 yrs.	1	$56,500
I	W	F	4.2 yrs.	7.0 yrs.	3.5 yrs.	2	$56,000
J	B	M	3.5 yrs.	5.0 yrs	1.5 yrs.	2	$56,000
K	H	F	4.7 yrs.	8 yrs.	3.0 yrs.	3	$55,500
L	A/PI	M	4.0 yrs.	7.0 yrs.	3.0 yrs.	3	$55,100
M	W	M	3.8 yrs.	7.1 yrs.	2.0 yrs.	2	$55,000
N	W	F	4.0 yrs.	6.5 yrs.	0.9 yrs.	3	$54,900
O	W	M	0.7 yrs.	0.7 yrs.	0.7 yrs.	2	$54,600
P	W	F	0.6 yrs.	0.6 yrs.	0.6 yrs.	3	$53,300
Q	A/PI	F	0.7 yrs.	0.7 yrs.	0.7 yrs.	3	$53,200

Figure 2: **SALARY GRADE 14 — MARKET ANALYSTS (SALARY RANGE $54,000-$61,000)**

In Figure 2, do any of the employees' salary situations give you cause for concern? While providing for the compensation principle of "differentiation among peers," a few items warrant a closer analysis.

- Employee A is paid above the maximum of the range. There may be lawful reasons for such, but a review of personnel files and a brief conversation with the human resource professional should prove illuminating. After identifying the rationale and assuming it was lawful (e.g., red-circling), ensure there were not others who were treated differently. To be credible, the justification must be lawful, fair and uniformly applied.

- Compare Employee D with Employees A, B and C. Can the $2,000 to $3,000 salary differential be explained? While it may not seem to be a large differential, combine it with a good rating and more time in job than two comparators and it should be flagged.

- Employee F stands out. She has the most seniority, time in grade and time in job and her performance is above average (rated 2). Is there something in her file that might justify the $5,000 differential with others in this title paid more?

- Employee K stands out. Her time in both grade and job do not account for the $6,500 differential with Employee A. Her performance is rated a 3. A review of her personnel file is warranted.

- It appears that the company hired externally into this job title within the past 12 months. Why is Employee O paid more than Employees P and Q? (You'll recall that a salary differential at time of hire is often impossible to overcome due to fiscal controls on salary increases.)

- Why are Employees P and Q paid below the salary minimum?

- Inasmuch as the company has a policy that all "new to grade" be rated a 3, 4 or 5 during the first review cycle, why is Employee O rated a 2? A review of the most recent performance evaluation and a discussion with human resources are advised.

- Employees K and L's personnel files should be reviewed. Is there a reason that these employees' salaries lag behind their peers? Are the rationales just?

At the lower salaries of the range, issues of initial placement and starting salary often emerge.

The available data for this matrix will be company-specific, due to database limitations and compensation components. One company may not have seniority in a database format; another company may track merit increases in addition to salary; while yet another may track all increases.

Such increases might be given for:

- Accelerated increase cycle to move employee closer to midpoint (salary progression)

- Compression

- Internal equity

- Market adjustment/competitive adjustment

- Retention/critical skill adjustment

- Salary range adjustment

- Skill-based pay increase

- Step rate or lump-sum increase.

In this instance, the matrix might look like the following:

ID	Race	Gender	Salary	Merit Increase	Other Increase	Perform. Rating	Time in Job	Time in Grade	Seniority

One might then sort this matrix by salary from highest to lowest paid. If no anomalies appear, re-sort the data by time in grade. Do any issues arise? Re-sort the data by time in job. Does this bear the closest semblance to pay? Does seniority affect pay at all?

Each time the analyses is conducted, a review of personnel files for those whose pay is questioned should be conducted. It could be that there are lawful reasons for salary discrepancies. A file review might also determine that salary adjustments are warranted.

Interestingly, while the OFCCP's investigator's manual, *The Federal Contract Compliance Manual,* has never contained specific guidance on how to determine compensation discrimination, this title-by-title analysis has been a tool widely accepted and used for the past 30-plus years. Some general interrogatives were added in the early 1990s for investigators conducting specific "glass ceiling" corporate management-level investigations as the agency's focus began to shift upward.

A Shift in Focus

In the early 1990s, things began to change — though the impetus often is debated. During that time federal investigators began grouping a variety of titles together for comparative salary purposes. Some blame, or credit, a specific person with the change. Others claim it was federal investigators' frustration with confronting a host of slightly varying titles when auditing companies for compliance with labor laws. In fact, a major workplace change during the 1980s and 1990s was the ballooning of person/position-specific job titles. This increase in new titles was one of the results of downsizing and re-engineering of the late 1980s and early 1990s. Whether the variety of titles was tied to the desire to accurately reflect responsibilities or technical skills, or as a reward by management, "to get more out of them," the ballooning did not go unnoticed.[24]

Regardless of the driving force, federal investigators began looking at job positions by the salary grade assigned by the employer. This salary grade grouping process became commonly referred to as comparable work — not to be confused with comparable worth, which shall be discussed later.

The most likely reason for this shift, however, was the emergence of the OFCCP's "Glass Ceiling Initiative." It was through that effort, which began in 1989 under the stewardship of then-Secretary of Labor Elizabeth Dole, that the OFCCP raised its sights from ensuring entry-level and mid-level nondiscrimination to every position in a work force.

During this initiative, the OFCCP began to review entire corporate work forces by salary grades or job levels. The OFCCP identified very few titles that were "exactly the same" for comparative purposes at mid and upper levels of most workplaces. While at large employers there may be 20 to 50 or more employees with the exact same title (i.e., customer service representative) at the upper levels of most companies, titles exist for a specific area or product line. For example, while there may be 20 vice presidents, they would be vice presidents of a product line, region or function. The same might hold true for titles such as assistant vice president and senior manager, as well.

These positions — though not identical — often are placed by the company's compensation division (with or without the assistance of outside consultants) into a series of salary grades. One's pay stub might include a salary code or similar marking denoting the pay range of one's job position. A typical salary structure consists of several job grades with corresponding pay ranges. To the OFCCP, titles placed within the same salary grade were ripe for comparison as the federal government itself has a structure of 15 salary grades each with 10 steps, and a separate executive management structure. Those within the federal government would agree that all those in their salary grade are their peer group, and an analysis and review of such would be appropriate. Though less controversial today, this remains a major contentious issue for the private sector.

If the OFCCP's "Glass Ceiling Initiative" was the driving force, it also would explain why that entity became the lead agency in this entire area of wage discrimination. Not only does it have proactive audit abilities, but it also has access to a vast amount of employment data from which to identify patterns. In the 1990s while the OFCCP was using this new approach using salary grades for comparison and garnering millions of dollars in back pay and salary adjustments each year, the EEOC produced roughly $1 million to

2 million in settlements of equal pay cases per year.[25] More recently, the
EEOC has adopted a similar methodology.

The Salary Grade: "We're All Peers Here"

This new approach using salary grades as the basis for compensation
comparisons made cogent sense. "By the very act of creating a grade level
system, where each employee has approximately the same potential to move
from the minimum to the maximum of his/her grade range dependent upon
performance, the employer has recognized that certain jobs are essentially
similar in terms of skill, effort, and responsibility," stated OFCCP officials.[26]

Situation A: An investigator at Company Zed might find 43 project
managers in the work force all identified in salary grade M-22. These
positions may or may not have the exact same specific area of oversight,
budget authority or personnel management, yet have been placed in the same
grade by the employer. Should the investigator review these positions as a
cluster? How should this be handled?

Answer: A good investigator would validate with the compensation
division that these positions all have the same pay range (minimum and
maximum) and are considered "peers" for the purposes of salary administration. Having determined such, the investigator would perform analyses of
all salaries within salary grade M-22 and placement patterns into and out of
the salary grade. The investigator not only would have an entire group (or
class) for review but a greater understanding of how individuals are being
treated within this salary grade.

The results have been startling. The comparison of how individuals are
actually compensated often diametrically opposes how a company *thinks* its
salary and rewards systems operate.

Situation B: A large customer service center is under a routine review by
the OFCCP. The federal investigator finds salary grade S-04 holds both the job
title Client Service Representative I and Client Service Representative II. Both
titles fall in the same salary grade with the same minimum salary, maximum
salary and midpoints. A review of job descriptions for these two titles does
not reveal any clear delineation of the two positions — leaving much to the
hiring manager's judgment. The investigator identifies 20 new hires into this
salary grade during the previous year. How should an investigator review this
salary grade?

Answer: A review of the job qualifications and salary grade placements might lead the investigator to believe there is no specific difference in individual job standards. The investigator also may establish that there is the appearance of a discriminatory pattern of salary grade placement affecting minority group members and/or women that warrants a closer examination of hiring files and personnel data. Such a review might not only consist of applicant files, personnel files and company testing, but also hiring-manager interviews.

Until recently, that investigator might have reviewed those hired into Client Service Representative I in isolation of those hired into Client Service Representative II. He or she most likely would have never reviewed those identified in the same salary grade as a group. Using the more recent salary grade approach of the OFCCP, the investigator would review all 20 hired into these positions within the same salary grade, as well as with regard to those already in the entire salary grade. Would management at your company be ready for such scrutiny?

The investigator might query:

- Bearing in mind that the job descriptions did not clearly identify the qualities or achievements a Client Service Representative II must possess vs. a Client Service Representative I, what did the hiring manager base his or her hiring and placement decisions upon?

- Were there "better qualified" people of color or women hired into Client Service Representative I than into Client Service Representative II?

- Is there a pattern of females or minorities with the same or more "relevant experience" than those in Client Service Representative II being placed in Client Service Representative I positions?

- What led to the differentiation in individuals' starting salaries?

The well-trained investigator would work to ensure that there is nondiscrimination in each salary grade with regard to initial hiring, job placement, starting salary, merit increases and promotional opportunity. While this may seem to be time-consuming and labor-intensive (often requiring a vast amount of filing), much of this time could be saved if management documented hiring and compensation decisions, and employers monitored these practices proactively. This is not to say there cannot be any dollar difference between individuals, but large variations should be legally sustainable.

The employer community has not warmly welcomed this salary grade approach. Many turned to the Internet and broadcast their views via Web sites claiming: *"OFCCP Revs Up Pay Disparity Issues"* or *"Pushing Back, Tips for Federal Contractors on Handling the OFCCP"* or *"Contractors Beware: OFCCP Targets Discrimination in Pay."*

"How can the OFCCP do this?" managers inquired. Corporate lawyers maintained, and continue to argue to this day, that such jobs are widely different and are not "substantially the same," therefore the Equal Pay Act cannot be invoked. The OFCCP has held firm. The OFCCP put forward that inasmuch as the employer (or its outside benchmarking firm) placed these jobs in the same salary grade, with the same salary minimum and maximum, then these were "comparable" for salary analyses. It was *not* an outside force determining comparability but each individual company determining such for itself.

Interestingly, it has been lawyers, not compensation experts, debating as to whether a salary grade was a suitable basis for comparison. Yet, according to compensation experts, "[a] grade is a grouping of different jobs that are considered substantially equal for pay purposes. Grades enhance an organization's ability to move people among jobs within a grade with no change in pay."[27] Thus, a salary grade analysis makes perfect sense ... to an extent. Should job titles be compared for salary purposes across business units? Should salary grades be compared for salary analysis across business units or product lines? These issues are still debatable.

Comparable Worth

A few points need to be made regarding the concept of "comparable worth." This concept emerged in the 1970s. The doctrine of comparable worth helped explain the wage gap between men and women. The doctrine asserted that employers and society undervalued jobs dominated primarily by women. The theory asserted that the continuation of such practices was discriminatory and that the courts should create wage parity with other positions not dominated by women.

In fact, the U.S. Commission on Civil Rights held hearings on this issue in the 1980s, which resulted in "Comparable Worth: Issue for the '80s." Since then, the theory of comparable worth has not gained much momentum.

What is comparable worth? According to WorldatWork, comparable worth refers to "the doctrine that men and women who perform work of the same 'inherent value' should receive similar levels of compensation.

According to this doctrine, jobs have an inherent value that can be compared across jobs of quite different content. Those accepting this position maintain that women performing jobs of comparable worth to those performed by men should be paid the same as men, excepting allowable differences (e.g., seniority plans, merit plans, production-based pay plans or different locations)."[28]

Several theories explain why individuals tend to cluster in low-wage jobs. Two competing views tend to focus on the choices minority group members and women make and the obstacles they face in the work force. The neoclassical human capital theory focuses on the investments individuals make in themselves (years of education, advanced degrees, job training, etc.) as the reason these groups do not hold higher-paying positions and are therefore paid less. This lower level of investment could be because of a myriad of factors, including the desire for greater flexibility in their lives precluding the investment. It bears noting, however, that this lower level of investment also could be caused by an employer's lack of providing adequate investment (on-the-job training, etc.). When an employer or employment practices preclude qualified minority group members or women, these acts may be discriminatory. The constraints theory focuses on exclusionary practices of job segregation.[29] Regardless of the reason for the clustering, the push for comparable worth appears to have subsided since the Supreme Court decision in this area.

In *Gunther v. Washington*, the only U.S. Supreme Court decision on comparable worth, the majority specifically avoided endorsement of the theory. While there has been very little court activity on comparable worth since that time, it has become a political football for interest groups and state-level politicians.

At present, the theory of comparable worth is not grounded in federal law; however, some state laws have incorporated these principles. The concept of comparable worth has consistently been an agenda item for women's groups and concerns. One reason the doctrine of comparable worth has not been accepted is that the courts have continuously upheld the use of market data as a valid rationale to pay different salaries for different jobs, even though the use of "market" has great subjectivity and variability when setting wages.

How comparable worth differs from the salary grade technique used by the federal government is simple. There is no outside trade association, women's group or law enforcement agency deciding which jobs are comparable in the OFCCP's approach. The proponents of comparable worth historically have articulated which positions predominantly held by women, and predominantly held by men, they felt should be comparable in salary. In the OFCCP's more conservative approach, it is the employer that determines which jobs are comparable, and the salary grade is what determines the compensation range. Thus, there may in fact be positions predominantly held by women in the same salary grade as positions predominantly held by men. How do their salaries stack up? What is the driving force behind marked salary differences? This is what the systemic approach attempts to determine.

The Systemic Approach: In General

In smaller entities, a title-by-title approach to review compensation might suffice. An entire salary grade could be reviewed in this fashion in many small workplaces. In larger entities, a more macro review of salary grades or job level should be conducted as well. After first reviewing such positions by exact title to ensure nondiscrimination, the prudent manager should review the entire work force salary grade by salary grade, or job level by job level. Though some may advocate reviewing salaries by EEO-1 job group as well, these seem much too macro and would generally not be relevant in a compensation review (though some investigators use this macro grouping for a first rough cut). These large EEO-1 job groupings include "Executives," "Professional" and "Technicians" and generally are too broad for comparative purposes.

Who to review and how to review salary grades or job levels for pay equity remain contentious issues. The issue with oversight agencies and commissions has not been that the wrong person was conducting compensation audits within the business sector, but rather that no one was doing so. Thus, the employer should decide who should perform such audits. Once the role is identified, the question becomes, how do you best audit base salary? The following steps are recommended for the employer trying to find the "safe haven" or bright-line test for pay equity.

Compensation systems tend to be quite complicated. Compensation practitioners pride themselves on developing systems that are unbiased, while also being responsive to the needs of management. These professionals maintain up-to-date credentials and keep abreast of what is happening in their industry, continually bringing forward new and innovative ways to compensate America's workers. While these individuals develop and monitor their systems for a host of business reasons, they are generally not responsible for ensuring the systems *operate* in a nondiscriminatory fashion. While the compensation professional generally has no corporatewide EEO responsibilities, these individuals appear to be in the perfect position to recommend strategies and analyses to ensure nondiscrimination in compensation. The closer one is to any one system, the more that person knows how to influence it. However, whoever takes the lead in ensuring the integration of EEO responsibilities with the compensation system(s) should consult with the compensation staff to ensure validity.

Notably, individuals who hold titles focusing on work force diversity generally have no access to compensation data. They usually focus on quality of work/life issues and "banding" of individuals for career development and upward mobility. It also bears noting that when companies group jobs together for diversity purposes, these bands generally do not correlate to compensation bands used by companies embracing broadbanding in compensation.

Though the workplace diversity staff has historically interfaced with some of the highest levels of management, these individuals generally operate outside all legal frameworks and mandates. This may be changing. Whether due to downsizing or management's realization that there might not be a drastic change in the demographics of its work force, there anecdotally appears to be a decrease in the staffing of diversity groups and units. In some cases, diversity responsibilities have been reassigned to the human resources and/or EEO staff. These individuals may now be responsible for both the legal EEO compliance of the employer as well as diversity data and quality of life issues. Though there may be some political fallout by removing diversity from an executive-level reporting relationship to the HR generalist or EEO director, there may be some economies of scale and increased productivity gains.

In most management scenarios, EEO concerns very few individuals who generate data and create reports on specific employment transactions. In most cases, base salary is the only compensation data in which the EEO officer has access. Generally, this individual will have very little interaction with the compensation experts and the systems being developed and implemented. Bringing together the compensation experts and the EEO officers would foster a greater understanding of nondiscrimination mandates — at a minimum. It also might bring synergy and a better way of doing business for both entities.

In fairness to federal and state investigators, compensation is one of the most difficult areas in which to ensure nondiscrimination in employment.

With nondiscrimination in compensation being only one of the mandates these investigators enforce, how can anyone expect investigators to know and understand the complexities of compensation the way a professional in the field might? While companies might use the same system or same wording, they actually may utilize the system in different fashions, and the wording may mean very different things to each company. As alluded to previously, training of federal investigators on the nuances of salary administration would be difficult, but not impossible. While proposed legislation in the 107th Congress would require such training, it would be quite a feat.

Unable or unwilling to understand the complexities of compensation systems, and oftentimes unable to gain access to the information needed to appropriately audit a company's compensation system, the OFCCP began auditing compensation with a broad brush approach. In fact, the majority of federal investigators does not delve into how an individual company's salary system operates at all, but grasps instead at rudimentary means to identify salary differences. In so doing, the government believes it can audit more companies more expeditiously. Using this rudimentary approach, an auditor will look deeper and much closer only if there is cause for concern. If this broad brush approach looks equitable, the agency will move on.

The Department of Labor has repeatedly stated its view of encouraging proactive self-analysis by employers. "The OFCCP strongly encourages federal contractors to conduct analyses of their compensation systems in accordance with the self-audit responsibilities under Executive Order 11246, to eliminate or prevent discriminatory policies and practices in this very important aspect of employment."[30] Why companies are not doing so remains a mystery.

A senior OFCCP manager once posed a question to me, "When I give speeches and remind companies that their proactive audit responsibilities include all forms of remuneration, they tell me they do not have anyone in their companies who can do this for them. When I respond that they could hire an outside consultant, they tell me, 'No thanks.' What gives?" While budgetary restraints could preclude the hiring of outside consultants, it also could be the desire to keep all information in-house. Or, it could be that there is a lack of desire on the part of some managers to fix or right things that an audit may identify.

While some might argue that there is no incentive to identify and fix compensation concerns proactively, I would argue that employee morale and public opinion should be enough of a driving force. Add to this equation that any problem remedied proactively may limit any findings of fault and back pay awards in the future.

Some will caution employers not to perform any compensation analysis before consulting a professional or attorney with experience in the area of compensation systems. Additionally, an employer should be prepared to remedy any concerns raised by such an internal audit, or any unlawful pay practices might be considered "intentional" and expose the employer to even greater liabilities.[31]

Given this risk-risk analysis, what should an employer do? Why perform such analyses if a company's chance of being audited is slim? First, it's the right thing to do. Second, employers have received a wake-up call that their compensation systems and accounting practices warrant closer scrutiny. Third, by conducting such on a routine basis, the compensation professional is in the lead position, not following. Finally, fairness is a basic tenet vital to attracting and retaining a strong work force. Therefore, review and analysis are recommended.

Whether the EEO staff, the compensation division, the HR generalist or outside compensation consultant competent in the areas of EEO conducts the analysis, it needs to be done. A review of one's compensations system(s) using the current federal investigators' techniques, as well as one based upon how the employer's compensation system(s) actually function(s), is advised. By doing so, an employer can gain confidence that its systems are functioning in a nondiscriminatory fashion.

Such analyses ought to be performed under "attorney-client privilege" and as a work product being prepared to meet the company's obligation to self-audit. By identifying and remedying salary issues proactively, and monitoring for such, an employer can send a signal to its work force that it cares about diversity where it counts most — in the paycheck.

As we learned when we were children, there are sins of commission and sins of omission. If one's company is a federal contractor, by failing to proactively audit one's system(s), one is failing to meet one's requirements to affirmatively ensure nondiscrimination in employment (a sin of omission). Even if one's company does not hold any federal contracts, it still would be prudent to ensure that one's workplace is free from such discrimination.

How should this be done? That will vary greatly from company to company. At a small employer, the title-by-title analysis may suffice. At a large employer, a systemwide audit is recommended as well. How should a large employer audit its pay practices? What exactly is the federal government's approach? And, if an employer conducts such, is it a safehaven? These are difficult questions to answer. Regrettably, it varies by region of the country, the quality of the individual investigator and the company's cooperation. In general, the federal government's compliance audits review only base pay and increases. In fact, the form government contractors are required to file (the OFCCP EO Survey) states:

For the purposes of this EO Survey, monetary compensation is defined as an employee's base rate (wage or salary) plus other earnings such as cost-of-living allowances, hazard pay, or other increment paid to all employees regardless of tenure on the job. Monetary compensation should not include the value of benefits, overtime, or one-time payments such as relocation expenses.

Upon return of this form, the OFCCP may perform any or all of several general broad brush analyses to determine if there is a systemic concern.

The following are general approaches. Analysis of base pay alone may be satisfactory for hourly workers or entry-level positions, but in most workplaces where other forms of remuneration are used, additional areas should be reviewed.

The Systemic Approach: How-To

The systemic approach has several steps, some or all of which may be performed by an investigative agency. While a poor audit by such an investigative body may not touch on all of these, a quality review would. It always is advantageous for the compensation professional to be ahead of the curve — to be in the driver's seat. It is with this premise that the compensation professional is encouraged to proactively audit the systems within his/her domain. Such an approach would encompass several analyses including:

- Shadow analysis (below and above the minimum/maximum)
- Mean (average) analysis
- Median analysis
- Outlier analysis (those beyond two standard deviations from the mean/median)
- Factor analysis

- Market rate analysis

- Regression analysis.

Note: In each of these analyses, the person reviewing the system is looking for patterns that might emerge (by salary grade or job level) that might be seen as discriminatory. That is to say, are there significant pay disparities that tend to favor Caucasians or men? The first analysis is a review of those who are outside the salary range.

Shadow Analysis

Employers that hire or promote minority group members or women into a salary grade and do not pay them the minimum of the salary range always amaze me. Shocking as it may seem to some, many employers do not even use the systems they have created. Why create a system with minimums and maximums if managers are allowed to routinely violate it? If the salary range for jobs in salary grade 1 is $13,500-$18,500, why would a manager hire someone at $12,500? Or $20,000?

While such pay practices are allowed (albeit often as "exceptions"), more often than not, it has been my experience that if there are individuals below the minimum of a salary grade…in the shadows … it is a minority group member or a woman. Similarly, it is also my experience that if there is someone outside the salary grade … in the shadows … on the upper end (above the maximum) it is a Caucasian. While some of those below the minimum may be due to a rapid promotional rate, and may in fact be a good thing, this is not always the case. Poor management oversight often is the cause.

This is a simple "first-cut" analysis. See the following example for the lowest-paid five salary grades at Workforce Zed.

Salary Grade	Minimum	Midpoint	Maximum
01	$11,500	$12,750	$14,000
02	$13,500	$15,250	$17,000
03	$16,300	$18,150	$20,000
04	$19,500	$21,750	$24,000
05	$23,800	$26,400	$29,000

When a spreadsheet format of salaries is produced, identification is made as to who falls below the minimum and above the maximum of each salary grade. Who are they? Why are they there?

Such an analysis might lead to the following results:

Salary Grade Race/Gender		Below the Minimum	Above the Maximum	
SG01	Black Male	$11,000	White Male	$14,500
	Asian Female	$10,800		
	Black Female	$10,500		
	Hispanic Male	$10,800		
	White Female	$11,300		
SG 02	Black Female	$13,300	White Male	$18,300
SG 03			Asian Male	$22,000
SG 04	White Female	$18,800		
	Black Female	$17,500		
SG 05	Black Male	$23,000	White Male	$31,000
			White Male	$33,000
			Black Male	$32,000

Some of these salaries might be appropriate, while others may warrant discussion and further analysis.

Example 1: If one has a *strictly enforced* policy of no salary increases above X percent, then a recently promoted minority group member or woman might fall below the minimum of the range (arguably others would fall there as well). This is especially true for individuals who have received a series of recent promotions. Salaries below the minimum often are referred to as "green circled."

Example 2: If Joe was demoted from a higher salary grade, his salary might be "red-circled" (held at the current level and not reduced) so as not to penalize him. Therefore, his salary might fall outside the maximum of the new, lower range. (Again, this would not be common, but a rare instance where jobs might be re-evaluated or demotions may occur.)

Example 3: There is concern with those newly hired into the lowest salary grade 01. Why were the only individuals being paid below the minimum minority group members or women? When the exceptions to the salary grade ranges are predominantly minority group members or women, a closer review is warranted.

When discussing "exceptions," it bears remembering that the more exceptions a company has to its compensation system and its rules, the more difficult it will be to argue that it has a system at all, much less one that operates in a non-discriminatory fashion. Salaries requiring adjustments for equity should occur prior to conducting any further macro analyses, so as not to further skew data.

Surprised to find a female executive below the minimum of the salary range, the company was questioned on why her salary was so low. The response was "she's been recently moved there for diversity purposes, and not fully performing the job." This stimulated further discussions as to whether she thought she was in "training" or fully performing the functions of the position; what "diversity purposes" meant to the company; what her job description actually read; and, the ramifications of equal pay laws. The company's response to many of these questions was vague, as was its knowledge of legal requirements. A salary adjustment was required.

Mean (Average) Analysis

After assuring that there are no deviations from the standards of the salary range that violate EEO mandates, several statistical analyses are used in an effort to identify salary trends or central tendencies. One such analysis is the mean (average) approach. Find the mean (average) for men/women, minority group members/Caucasians within each salary grade and look for "trends" with regard to salary disparities. The mean is the sum of all the salaries in the salary grade, divided by the number of individuals in the salary grade.

The mean salary of men is the sum of all men's salaries in the grade divided by the number of males. The mean salary of women in the salary grade is the sum of all the women's salaries in the grade divided by the number of women, etc. (See Figures 3A, 3B and 3C.)

A similar analysis would be conducted for minority group members and Caucasians. Simple computer programs can do the same. After doing so, the investigator looks for trends using the means of the salary grades and might question:

- Are women paid less on average than men at every salary grade?

- Are women paid less on average than men at most salary grades?

FIGURE 3A: SALARY GRADE A RANGE ($24,000-$29,000)				
$23,500	$23,800	$24,000	$24,000	$25,000
$25,000	$25,200	$25,400	$25,500	$25,500
$25,700	$25,900	$26,000	$26,000	$26,400
$26,600	$26,700	$28,000	$28,100	$28,300
$28,400	$28,500	$29,000	$29,000	$29,500

Mean of Salary Grade A: Although two of the salaries are below the minimum and one is above the maximum, assuming these are valid exceptions which do not need adjustments, they should be included in the analysis. The sum of the salaries is $659,000. The mean is $659,000/25 = $26,360.

FIGURE 3B: SALARIES OF MEN WITHIN SALARY GRADE A			
$23,500	$24,000	$25,000	$25,400
$25,500	$25,900	$26,000	$28,000
$28,100	$29,000	$29,000	$29,500

Mean (Men) of Salary Grade A: $318,900/12 = mean of $26,575

FIGURE 3C: SALARIES OF WOMEN WITHIN SALARY GRADE A			
$23,800	$24,000	$25,000	$25,200
$25,500	$25,700	$26,000	$26,400
$26,600	$26,700	$28,300	$28,400 and $28,500

Mean (Women) of Salary Grade A: $340,100/13 = mean of $26,162

- Are minority group members paid less on average than Caucasians at every salary grade?

- Are minority group members paid less on average than Caucasians at most salary grades?

- Is there no cause for concern at lower salary grades but great concern at higher salary grades?

- At the entry levels, do newly hired females/minority group members being paid less than men/Caucasians cause the disparity?

Median Analysis

The analysis of salaries by median in each salary grade is similar to that of means. The median is *the* most central salary in each range for each group being analyzed. Using the same salaries as the example, the median salary for men would be compared with the median salary of women, and the median salary for Caucasians would be compared with that of minority group members.

During an audit, employers often will offer median salary analyses to an investigator as they may portray the company in a better light. This is due to the fact that the median is more closely aligned to central tendencies and does not reflect the extreme highs and lows of the salary grade that the average would include. It would be better if companies proactively reviewed their systems using either approach to ensure nondiscrimination — and ideal if they used both. As previously mentioned, before any macro analyses are conducted, care should be taken to group individuals by proper status — removal of part-time employees (or conversion of their wages to a full-time rate), removal of consultants or working retirees and contractors who are not on the company's payroll, and removal of any other individuals who might skew the accuracy of such analyses. It should be pointed out that while the mean and median are macro rudimentary data analyses, they do give a starting point for both a company and an investigator.

After identifying the mean and/or median of each grade level, a review for "patterns" is conducted. Is there anything one can glean from this data? Are minority group members consistently paid less than Caucasians at every level of the company's work force? Is there relative equity at the lower salary grades, but huge variations in the upper levels?

Outlier Analysis: Statistically Significant Differences
Another approach at identifying "the most egregious" salary issues is to determine just how great a difference there is in salaries within a salary grade. This approach is to measure the dispersion of salaries from the mean/median in each grade. The outlier analysis of standard deviation from the mean or median may be performed to identify how far individual salaries fall from the center tendency. Generally, any salaries falling outside two standard deviations would be questioned. A test of statistical significance could follow.

In layman's terms, these steps will determine if the salary differences are so great that they could not have occurred by chance. If so, an investigator might assert the probable cause of discrimination. To those conducting proactive internal audits, this approach is helpful in identifying salaries that warrant a closer look. Though every federal investigator does not uniformly use this approach, it is a helpful tool. Any salaries that fall outside these ranges will generally be the same salaries identified ("flagged") in later analyses. For example, a few extremely low salaries of women or minority group members (outside two standard deviations from the mean) also may affect the mean analysis in such a way as it too is questioned. Thus, it is advisable to identify those salaries that are "outliers" early and ensure there are nondiscriminatory, valid, consistent reasons for such variations. If any of these salaries need adjustments, these should be performed prior to any further analysis. It should be noted that many of these flagged salaries already should have been identified in the below the minimum/above the maximum analysis.

Factor Analysis: Correlation with Other Employment Variables
It is far better to be knowledgeable enough to be able to explain your system than to try to explain away its problems.

After obtaining the mean/median salaries by job level or salary grade, an investigator often tries to couple this information with data that could explain the differences. Curiously, this often is done without consulting the company. The OFCCP has stated:

"One of the biggest hurdles to overcome is identifying variables that substantially influence compensation, that are related to productivity or worth, and that are not potentially tainted by discriminatory decisions of the employer, e.g. performance ratings, promotions, etc. There is infinity of variables that *could* affect compensation. Based on the experience of OFCCP to date, the variables which substantially influence compensation are time with the company, time at job level, performance on the job, education and prior experience before being hired by the company ...." (Update on Systemic Compensation Analysis, Overview, undated.)

Figure 4: MOST INFLUENTIAL FACTOR AFFECTING SALARIES — TIME IN GRADE			
Salary Grade B			
Average Salary Men	$35,400	Average Time in Grade	3.3 yrs.
Average Salary Women	$31,200	Average Time in Grade	2.8 yrs.
Average Salary Caucasians	$33,450	Average Time in Grade	3.0 yrs.
Average Salary Minorities	$29,300	Average Time in Grade	2.9 yrs.

The investigator would expect to find some relationship between the salary information and other variables. There is enormous variability in what an investigator will review and find "meaningful." In Figure 4, the company has stated that time in grade is the most influential factor affecting salaries within a grade level. Thus, an investigator might compare the salaries found in Salary Grade B with average (or median) time in grade level.

- Does the fact that the average male time in grade is 0.5 years longer than the average female time in grade explain the $4,200 difference in salaries? Will the investigator think so? Or, will he or she state this is too great a dollar difference for such a short time in grade variation?

- With average time in grade so close, will the average salary of minority group members being $4,150 less than that of Caucasians raise a red flag?

- Are there other variables that can explain these differences? Does the company have numerical performance ratings? Will a review of these help explain these differences?

When the compensation professional runs the average or median analysis by grade, and marries the data with the factor he/she believes should affect pay, there often is cause for concern. This leads to additional analyses. It could be that time in grade is more of a determining factor at lower salary grades than at higher salary grades, especially if there is a bulk of external hiring being conducted at the most senior levels. It could be that the company's official misspoke when she said that seniority is a driving force in pay, when in fact most of the dollar difference disappears when both time in grade and current performance are considered. It cannot be stressed enough how very important it is for employers to be able to explain their system and the variables that affect compensation *before* having to defend salary differences or "explain away" an investigator's concerns. This is a very important distinction.

When faced with macro salary disparities, an employer may be able to justify such by disclosing how his or her system actually operates. Conversely, if an employer is not familiar with his or her system and is not reviewing it for nondiscrimination, he or she may find that what was thought to be driving salaries at the company actually is not.

Example: An employer may state that performance and corresponding ratings are the No. 1 variables affecting salary in each salary grade. Yet, when a review of actual ratings is performed (and reviewed against base salaries by the investigator), the employer may find that while minority group members or women are rated higher, they are in fact not being compensated at the higher levels or with higher rates of increase. When presented with this, the manager often struggles to find other variables to "explain away" differences. "Did I say performance? I meant performance and ratings and …."

Many lawyers will assert that "the mere existence of a disparity between pay earned by men and women, even if the jobs are the same, does not alone establish a *prima facie* case of a Title VII violation because such a disparity does not give rise to an inference of an intent to discriminate."[32] While it may not show intent to discriminate, it may indicate a pattern of discriminatory actions at that company. Any salary grades or job levels for which an explanatory job-related correlation cannot be identified (e.g., mean time in grade) should be investigated fully.

This scenario is similar to *Houses of Parliament* by the great Impressionist painter Claude Monet. Up close one sees dark hues and a series of brush strokes. It is not until one steps back from the painting that the structure of Parliament reveals itself. Similarly, individual managers make a host of individual compensation decisions annually, but it is not until one takes an overall view of those decisions rolled up into a more macro unit, department or division that a pattern might emerge. It is the totality of these individual decisions that warrants discussion. If the individual brush strokes (salary decisions) are proper, a beautiful work of art may result. If not ….

"At a prior employer the new female college graduates were being hired at a lower salary level than the males, almost uniformly," stated the female systems analyst. After a few years of grousing about this fact and the general treatment of women, she decided to leave. "I was immediately offered a 2 salary grade pay bump to stay. Now you know that there must have been funny business going on with my salary if they could offer me a 2 grade increase just like that to stay."

This type of vignette was reaffirmed in testimony offered by Susan Bianchi-Sand, Executive Director of the National Committee on Pay Equity. "Women who hold bachelor degrees earn only $2,190 more per year than white men who have never taken one college course, and $12,316 less than college educated white men," she stated.[33] Compensation practitioners will uniformly swear that they have developed a nondiscriminatory system: one that allows management to differentiate among peers and appropriately reward performance. *But*, these same officials will not swear that managers in the company are using the system in a nondiscriminatory fashion.

Though the OFCCP has taken the lead in spearheading compensation audits, in recent years the EEOC, though complaint-driven, has followed suit. The EEOC has published extensive guidance for its investigators in this area.

Market Rate Analysis

While small employers may not use a salary grade structure the way a large employer might, many mid-sized companies use market references for salary determinations. Market pricing is the setting of pay structures almost exclusively through matching pay for a very large percentage of jobs with rates paid in the external market.[34] Many data services offer surveys of salaries, average salary increases, bonus amounts and bonus as a percent of salary by job title and level.

If using a market rate approach, after determining the market rate for job, how do minorities and women fare? By job title, what percentage of the market rate do minority group members receive? Caucasians? How about men vs. women? In this setting, analyses, similar to those mentioned earlier for mean/median salary grade, are encouraged using the market rates or market reference points identified for each position.

Multiple Regression Analysis

> "My first job after graduate school was to statistically prove that women at a particular employer were not paid less nor disproportionately steered into dead-end jobs. No matter how I cut the data, I couldn't prove it. The numbers just weren't there."
>
> — *Female Analyst*

Having discussed the current state of pay with regard to broad-brush investigations by the federal government, the current case law in this area is predominantly founded upon the use of multiple regression analysis. This is a statistical technique that allows one to assess how one or more independent variables might affect the dependent variable — in this case, pay. A test for statistical significance then is added to these results. For example, using a multiple regression analysis, one might be able to show how performance and time in grade have a direct correlation to base pay. Unfortunately, for other employers, even when every possible variable is included in such an analysis, pay differentials remain.

One of the problems for managers, employers, and federal and state governments is that in some instances, data are not centralized in a database that readily lends itself to a multiple regression analysis. Thus, to disprove a discrimination claim, massive and laborious data entry must take place.

Additionally, outside assistance often is required for multiple regression analyses to be conducted properly. While this sounds easy, contrary to popular belief, there is not one "appropriate" formula for performing such analyses. Not only are the variables to be included in a multiple regression analysis often of dispute, some argue that the analyses should not be conducted within salary grades at all, but rather that the salary grade itself is an independent variable due to its subjectivity.

For all of these reasons, the introduction of regression analysis into an ongoing investigation often will result in a debate being undertaken by industrial psychologists and statisticians, rather than by HR practitioners, compensation analysts, lawyers or investigators. What variables should be included, which ones should not and who is the proper person to conduct such analyses are contested. Simply *alleging* that legitimate factors might explain away salary differences does not suffice in a court of law. If such cases go to court, the judge must determine the validity of the factors and the type of analysis conducted.

To avoid this situation, the rudimentary approaches mentioned earlier allow the investigator to perform a cursory review of many more companies without moving to a judicial setting. Further investigation is warranted and additional data requested only when these broad-brush approaches highlight concerns. While many large companies in the private sector have reluctantly accepted these approaches as the "tonic of the day," others will challenge them. An entire cottage industry has even emerged to meet this demand for analysis; a variety of software packages are available to perform these analyses.

Lawyers Critical of Systemic Approach

As discussed earlier, this systemic approach to salary analysis has not been without its detractors — the most vocal of which are lawyers. Though there are many such criticisms, in fairness to the legal profession, it is worth noting a few:

- **Dissimilar jobs:** Prior to this salary grade analysis, federal government reviews focused on exact same title. The current salary grade analysis compares jobs that may not be substantially the same.

- **Intent:** The federal government's approach does not meet the legal standard of intent to discriminate.

- **Specific practice:** This approach does not identify a specific practice that leads to any such pay disparities.

- **Undetermined factors:** This approach does not account for the entire myriad of factors that can affect one's base pay.

- **Statistically significant:** Differences in salary may not be statistically significant.

Some of these issues have merit. Others, such as disallowing the salary grade for comparative purposes, may not. As stated earlier, if jobs within a salary grade are considered substantially equal for pay purposes and allow greater flexibility for job transitions within grade, such an analysis is ideal. The variability lies in determining the most appropriate methodology.

Compensation Manuals

What does your company's compensation manual state with regard to internal equity in compensation? Does it discuss the principles of red-circling and green-circling? Does it allow deviations from the salary range? Does it discuss how to tie pay to performance? Does it give a good description of the principles of nondiscrimination? What does the manual state regarding documentation to justify decisions? Does the it discuss all forms of remuneration?

A good manual would form a road map for an internal audit or a review by an outside investigative body. A poor or obsolete manual would bear no semblance to how employees are compensated at present. While HR generalists and hiring managers might be able to identify the qualities and criteria that lead to initial salary differentials, and others might be able to describe the criteria for variations in performance ratings, is there a single source for this information? Is there uniformity and clarity across the work force? Is there cause for concern?

An Alternate Systemic Approach

After conducting a self-audit using the systemic approaches mentioned earlier, is it possible to review your compensation system using a company-specific method? While pay across an entire work force by salary grade is interesting, would it make more sense to refine the salary grade analysis by cost centers or business units? What is the most appropriate methodology at your company?

At one company, an audit by quartiles within each salary grade might be the most appropriate form of self-audit. Reviewing the demographics of each quartile coupled with corresponding compensation and time in title might be the most appropriate methodology. At another company, review of the salary increases might suffice. Yet at other companies a review of compa-ratios might be the most appropriate form of review. The compa-ratio is the relationship between how management pays its employees against the midpoint of that range.[35]

Compa-ratio = Average Rates Actually Paid vs. Range Midpoint

A compa-ratio of less than 1.0 implies that the employees on average are being paid less than the midpoint. A compa-ratio of greater than 1.0 would infer that the employees are being paid at rates higher than intended. This could be due to a host of factors. In this scenario, unusually high and low compa-ratios would require further review and analysis.

Today a host of companies tie base salary and bonus together to form a total cash pool. Those who have embraced this practice shake their heads in disbelief when base salary is requested during an OFCCP audit. How could the federal government request only base salary? Do they *really* want only base salary data, when the big discretionary money is in the bonus?

When managing total cash compensation, both components (base + bonus) may have targets and limits, or there may be a joint limit for the two in tandem. This total cash approach allows management greater flexibility to reward top performers or key employees, especially if limits are set on the amount of increase an employee may receive in base salary. The bonus is used as a part of incentive pay. A Towers Perrin study (1999) revealed that high performing companies did not pay extremely high salaries. In fact, "high performing companies are no more likely to pay above average salaries than other companies …. High performing companies lead the way in providing total cash compensation packages to their employees … via incentive pay." Such payments are generally tied to performance goals or are an inducement to take or remain on a specific project. In these instances, both components must be audited to ensure nondiscrimination. If separate performance rating/ranking systems are used, these too must be reviewed.

It is highly recommended that employers audit their compensation systems for nondiscrimination. Regardless of the approach taken by outside auditors, a review of compensation using the company's system is critical to accurately ensure fairness.

5

Broadbanding —
The Present and the Future?

"Discrimination is against the interests of business ... yet businesspeople often practice it. In the end, the costs are higher, less real output is produced and the nation's wealth accumulation is slowed."

— Federal Reserve chairman Alan Greenspan
in a speech to the National Community Reinvestment Coalition

In the past decade, while lawyers and lobbyists debated the principles of equality and fairness, access to data and how base salary should be audited, compensation analysts began to compress traditional salary grades into large salary bands. This practice, referred to as broadbanding, has become very popular with large employers. At the time of printing, broadbanding is under consideration at many companies, in metamorphosis at others and fully operational at others. This practice poses a host of pay equity issues.

We keep circling back to "Why should I audit my payroll?" For starters, it always is better to know one's weaknesses and address them head-on than have them identified publicly. A proactive review of compensation to ensure internal equity also is important because so many working Americans rely on their salary to meet day-to-day expenses. If there are any internal equity concerns in a salary grade structure, broadbanding may only exacerbate these flash points. Knowing what broadbanding is, and how it might affect your organization, is important for management and critical for the compensation professional.

Historically, at many large corporations, salary grades are numerous (often more than 15) with a relatively small dollar margin from minimum to maximum. While the administration of salaries (e.g., market surveys, benchmarking of positions, internal equity assessments, external equity assessments, etc.) can be quite time-consuming and a large share of any HR division's workload, federal and state investigators can easily analyze a grade structure, as it mirrors their own.

Broadbanding compresses these salary grades into a smaller number of pay bands. Broadbanding generally takes two forms:

Broad grades. These new structures usually have slightly fewer grades with larger spreads, often maintaining the traditional midpoints, quartiles and other salary grade characteristics.

Career bands. These usually very large broadbands have a very small number of bands representing significant "career changes." Companies using these broadbands may have as few as four bands in a work force setting and have a pay range spread in excess of 100 percent. Other companies' broadbands may have no ranges at all — no minimums, midpoints or maximums. (See Figure 5.)

For simplicity's sake, Company ABC did not overlap salaries between any of the macro pay bands, and job titles have been placed within the large bands in an exclusive fashion. Considering this example: A Company ABC manager had a $4,500 spread by which to differentiate among employees in Salary Grade 1 in the past. In the new system, that same manager has $15,500 at his or her discretion for the same positions. Can that manager use the entire band? In some companies, "Yes." At other companies where there are controls within the bands (i.e., certain jobs fall within certain quartiles) the answer may be, "No." This variability,

FIGURE 5: COMPANY ABC'S SALARY GRADE STRUCTURE	
Grade 1	($14,500-$19,000)
Grade 2	($16,000-$21,000)
Grade 3	($18,000-$24,000)
Grade 4	($22,000-$30,000)
Grade 5	($26,000-$40,000)
Grade 6	($30,000-$55,000)
Grade 7	($39,000-$65,000)
Grade 8	($45,000-$70,000)
Grade 9	($50,000-$80,000)
Grade 10	($70,000-$85,000)
Grade 11	($80,000-$95,000)
Grade 12	($90,000-$110,000)

Company ABC decides to broadband these grades to 4 large "career bands." A movement from Band 1 to 2 would be a career change and may require greater competencies and perhaps additional training. Company ABC's new pay and career band structure might look like this:

Band 1	($14,500-$30,000)
Band 2	($30,000-$55,000)
Band 3	($55,000-$70,000)
Band 4	($70,000-$110,000)

company by company, is the major reason that development of an exact "How to Audit" a compensation plan is virtually impossible.

While most companies use the same general terminology — broadbanding, pay for performance, total cash compensation, etc. — each company implements these terms in a slightly different fashion, often taking into account company culture, business sector and product line.

Driving Forces Behind Broadbanding

General Electric has been credited with being a bellwether in this area. GE reportedly led the way in reducing organizational levels, developing broad career bands and pay zones as part of its "Work-Out" delayering during the 1980s.[36] Others soon followed suit. While compensation specialists warn that broadbanding is not for every company, it does not take long for one company to influence the next. While dynamic organizations appear to be the best fit for such a system, many more rigid hierarchical companies have undertaken broadbanding as well. Some companies that have fully adopted the concept maintain it met their needs for a quicker, more flexible system that rewards risk taking. Others have embraced it for simplicity's sake alone.

Some companies may move to bands that are two to three traditional salary grades wide for economies of scale and streamlining of operations. Others, with bands as large as five to six traditional salary grades in width, may reduce the number of grades to embrace cultural change and greater adaptability.

With so many companies now global in nature, there is even greater interest in broadbanding. By broadbanding all of a company's operations (both in the United States and worldwide), a company gains flexibility in moving managers and executives worldwide. It makes brilliant sense for business planning, career development and compensation administration for certain companies to broadband their work forces.

Though there is this global shift with many U.S. companies, compensation experts warn that while employers may think globally, administration of broadbanding and other compensation practices likely would be better administered at the local level. What works in one country may not in another. In fact, while it may be that global companies have seized upon broadbanding to simplify compensation worldwide, it has not been without headaches. A few issues of concern are the quality of compensation survey data outside of the United States, and the cultural differences between the United States and other countries.[37]

In addition to globalization, the driving forces for such macro banding have included:

- Cross-fertilization across business lines and units (especially as companies downsized during the 1990s)
- Career development among employees
- Removal of the strict hierarchical structure that salary grades create
- Greater latitude in compensation determination
- Reduction in the workload that salary grade administration and job evaluation processes produce.

Pay Bands vs. Diversity Bands

It is important to note that broadbanding is *not* the same as diversity banding. In the last 15 years, many companies, having embraced diversity as a goal, began grouping their work forces into macro bands and reviewing them for diversity purposes. These diversity bands often form the basis of how well the company believes it is doing at hiring and promoting from a diverse talent pool. After grouping job titles into these macro diversity bands, companies then benchmark or formulate "diversity scorecards" for business units and management. There also may be efforts to tie these diversity scorecards to bottom-line profit margins and strategic planning. For the most part, these diversity bands are developed in isolation and do not mirror compensation bands. In fact, they generally are *not* developed, administered or reviewed by the same group of individuals within the company. As stated earlier, diversity efforts generally focus on hiring and promotion, "inclusivity" and career development ... not compensation.

Thus, the same company may embrace compensation broadbanding and diversity banding. These bands generally do not marry perfectly, if at all. Some titles may form the highest diversity band, but be in the second tier of the compensation band structure. (See Figure 6.)

In this example, no job titles are split between compensation bands or diversity bands. This is a very simplified version of a large work force. In reality, those charged with diversity or compensation might place the same title in several different bands. For example, the title "vice president" might be in found in several compensation bands, yet in only one diversity band.

And we wonder why our managers are so confused.

FIGURE 6: HR BANDING — DIFFICULTIES IN RELATING		
JOB TITLES*	**Diversity Band**	**Compensation Band**
1 – 17	Band A	Band 1
		Band 2
18 – 29	Band B	Band 3
		Band 4
		Some inclusion in Band 5
30 – 45	Band C	Some inclusion in Band 5
		Some inclusion in Band 6
		Some inclusion in Band 7
46 – 70	Band D	Balance of bands 6, 7 and all of 8

*Titles are numbered for simplicity's sake.

"Am I supposed to be tracking employees and career progressions by titles?"

"Should I be monitoring by diversity bands at all?"

"How do I marry these bands with compensation bands?"

"Which 'goals' will affect my salary if I don't meet them?"

And you think you're confused now … what if you were the corporate compliance officer who is required by law to create and monitor an affirmative action plan that requires bands (called job groups) to ensure nondiscrimination? Which data would you submit?

The affirmative actions plans (required by more than 90,000 U.S. establishments that hold contracts with the federal government) set guidelines for grouping of jobs and require goal settings when broad hiring and placement rates aren't met. The jobs are grouped by macro EEO-1 job groupings. Yet, more often than not, these plans are not even consulted when developing broad compensation bands or diversity bands. And which, if any, of these band groupings are required by law and routinely audited by federal investigators? Affirmative action plans, EEO-1 job categories, AAP job groups, job titles, salary grades, diversity bands, compensation bands. Can't we do better than this? Shouldn't there be a more streamlined, cohesive manner of monitoring one's employment patterns?

The obvious answer is "Yes." But, just as the news reports that the federal government's departments and agencies haven't been working well together and sharing information, the same rings true with our corporate divisions and departments. Shouldn't the compensation staff ensure their efforts correlate to the EEO staff's legal requirements? Shouldn't the diversity staff be required to ensure their banding efforts don't conflict with other bands and groupings within the same entity? Ideally, the baseline should be, "What is the legal standard we must meet?" If there were better coordination between these entities, not only would there be greater understanding of each other's mandates, but perhaps a better way of doing business.

Auditing Compensation in the Broadbanding Environment

Reviewing one's broadbanding compensation structure is perhaps more crucial than auditing a salary grade structure. While there is nothing intrinsically discriminatory about broadbanding, there is a concern that these broad ranges may need greater oversight and vigilance to ensure nondiscrimination. While some may argue that this vigilance could run directly counter to the fluid, flexible environment management desires, it can be effortless if done in a cohesive fashion.

"How can the virtues of paying for performance and flexibility be achieved in such a regulatory environment?"

"How can a company accurately audit for nondiscrimination in this new 'broad' environment?"

"Regardless of how my company self-audits, how will the federal government audit companies utilizing broadbanding?"

(See Figure 7 for general pay equity approaches that should be used in a broadbanding environment.)

Inasmuch as broadbanding means different things to different employers, it is critical that, just as in salary administration, each company review its bands in a company-specific manner. A pay analysis in the broadbanding environment should begin with the job-by-job review using the cohort matrix of pay patterning discussed in Chapter 4. This is the finest cut of salary information available. Just as in the salary grade analysis, this matrix should be shared with appropriate HR professionals (e.g., those assigned to that

FIGURE 7: **GENERAL PAY EQUITY APPROACHES**
Job-by-Job Review (Cohort Matrix of Pay Patterning)
Zone or Quartile Analysis
Band Analysis (Using the Salary Grade Approaches)
Multiple Regression Analysis by Broadband

business unit, etc.), preferably under the protections of attorney-client privilege and attorney-client work product. After reviewing such and ensuring there are valid reasons for pay differences (and remedying salary concerns warranting adjustments), the next analysis in the broadbanding environment will vary from one company to the next.

While there may be multitudinous job titles within the same broadband at some companies, in many there appears to be the beginning of a reversal in trends concerning titles. The desire to individualize very job-specific titles may be on the decline. Some companies actually have reduced the number of titles they use. While the employee may have external titles (on business cards, etc.), titles inside the company may have become more generic. "We encourage using internal titles for purposes of job code assignments, position matching for surveys, etc., but (we) do allow business card titles for external use," according to one respondent on a recent broadbanding survey.[38] If there are internal titles for survey matching and job code assignments, are these the most appropriate groups to review en masse in these companies? Do these jobs sharing the same title require the same skill, effort and responsibility and have the same working conditions?

Subset Analysis by Zone, Quartile or Family

Some employers, even though they've institutionalized broadbands, may follow a traditional salary administration approach by zones, job families or quartiles for jobs within each band. After completion of the job title cohort matrix of pay patterning, an audit using the appropriate unit — quartile, job family or zone — should be performed. Since the jobs in that subset or zone have the same salary range (and may have been a salary grade prior to broadbanding), they are an appropriate group for comparative purposes. Median, mean and outlier analyses should be conducted by this appropriate subset as well. (See Figure 8.)

In this case, one would begin by reviewing all of those in job title 1 as a group using the cohort matrix of pay patterning. For this example, job titles 1 to 33 can only be paid in the first quartile. There may be no deviations. The average/median salaries of men and women, Caucasians and minority group members within this quartile would be reviewed to ensure nondiscrimination and salary correlation with other lawful variables. Bear in mind, regardless of how the system was designed, if titles deviate from the salary quartile to which they are assigned, one quickly loses the ability to argue the quartile as an appropriate grouping for data analysis. Even if the company's compen-

FIGURE 8: SALARY BAND C (RANGE $45,300-$75,000)			
$45,300-$52,500	$52,500-$60,200	$60,200-$68,000	$68,000-$75,000
Title 1	Title 34	Title 56	Title 81
Title 2	Title 35	Title 57	Title 82
↓	↓	↓	↓
Title 33	Title 55	Title 80	Title 100

sation manual states that title and respective salaries may not deviate from a given range, if a pattern arises that deviates, the subset analysis loses credibility.

Band Analysis

The more deviations from the rule, the less a compensation system can be argued. In many instances, the system is violated so often the entire band becomes the group for comparative purposes. When this happens, there is the real possibility of a finding of even greater liability and discrimination. The small salary differences of a subset approach ($7,200 in Zone 1) are replaced by the potential for very large salary fluctuations (almost $30,000 in Band C) when broadbanding is used. Couple this with the fact that time in grade (which may have closely correlated with salary in a grade structure) is lost when a broadbanding environment is adopted. Thus, there is the need for greater oversight to ensure pay equity in a broadbanding environment.

What about the company that has fully embraced macro banding and sets no maximums, minimums, quartiles, zones or other means of sub-grouping its employees? How should that company audit its bands? In addition to a routine salary analysis by title, such a company should perform reviews by the entire band, and be prepared for large dollar differences and the reasons behind them. These are factors that an outside investigative body will inspect.

Using the entire band, conduct the mean (average) analysis, median analysis, shadow analysis and variable correlation analysis discussed earlier. Be sure to remedy any salary concerns warranting adjustments. Be prepared to provide lawful justifications for any macro pay differentials identified by an analysis of the entire band.

Business Unit Analysis

Perhaps it makes the most sense at your company to move directly from a macro establishmentwide band analysis to a business unit band analysis prior to any further refinements within the broadbands. The movement from an establishmentwide broadband approach to a smaller subset is predicated upon how salaries are set, how jobs are placed into the bands, budgetary constraints and how salaries are determined within the band.

For any company that has embarked on broadbanding, it is imperative to:

- Identify the most appropriate manner by which to review

- Build in self-auditing analyses (for internal equity) and begin using them well before an investigation or EEO charge.

Multiple Regression Analysis

For the company that has fully embraced broadbanding, a multiple regression analysis may be the best approach to ensuring pay equity. Inasmuch as numerous titles now reside in a single band with a large dollar difference, a thorough multiple regression analysis (discussed earlier) may be the only way to adequately audit one's system on a macro level.

Promotional Activity Using Broadbanding

Promotional activity plays a direct role in how individuals are compensated. The "fast track" in career advancement generally means better assignments, a higher salary and other forms of compensation, as well as a shorter time in title/position or grade. In a typical salary grade structure, promotional activity between standard salary grades may be tied to a successful business line, outstanding performance or even exemplary work on a special project, task force or report. When standard salary grades are compressed into broadbands, promotional activity between bands becomes more Herculean.

What must an employee achieve to make the leap? While movement within a salary grade might be a "step" and movement between standard salary grades a "jump," movement from one band to the next appears to be an enormous leap. Ensuring that such promotions or "leaps" are fair is important to ensuring financial fairness in the broadbanding arena. (See Figure 9.)

In this example, a review of the standard salary grades revealed women and minority group members clustered at the top of salary ranges for salary grades 9 and 12. When salary grades are compressed into broadbands, these same individuals appear at the high end of the salary ranges for the new bands C and D. While these individuals will not stand out as salary concerns in the broadbanding arena, ensuring that these same individuals have a level playing field for promotions to the next band becomes a management concern.

FIGURE 9: COMPRESSING 15 STANDARD SALARY GRADES INTO 5 BROAD PAY BANDS		
Salary Grades 1-3	to	Band A
Salary Grades 4-6	to	Band B
Salary Grades 7-9	to	Band C
Salary Grades 10-12	to	Band D
Salary Grades 13-15	to	Band E

When promotions from one band to the next are not based upon quantifiables (such as sales), but upon more subjective qualities (such as leadership or potential), closer scrutiny is warranted. What performance must be shown before individuals can be promoted from one band to the next? Are such performance measures or criteria captured in HR manuals? Are managers required to document these measures or qualities? Is anyone in HR charged with reviewing for nondiscrimination on a "spot check" basis? If these practices were well coordinated, there would be greater assurances that promotional activity is fair and that internal equity exists in compensation.

Total Cash Compensation

Many companies that have embarked on broadbanding also have embraced a total cash pool approach to compensation. Whatever the format (e.g., pay for performance, incentive pay, etc.), companies are embracing the union of base salary and bonus with much enthusiasm. By pooling both forms of cash, a manager has more discretion to award those who are outperforming the pack, and send clear signals of dissatisfaction to others. While appropriate review has been mentioned previously with regard to salary grades, it is even more important in a broadbanding environment. The same internal equity approach should be taken for each component individually and routinely reviewed.

Federal Investigations: A Mixed Lot

How have federal investigators dealt with broadbanding issues at companies reviewed to date? Private sector companies with a broadbanding structure report mixed results during federal government investigative audits. For some companies, the move to broadbanding was so recent that they simply backed out the jobs to the prior year's salary grade structure for the auditor, rather than educate him or her on the compensation system. In so doing, they avoided any discussions and analysis by pay band and were able to show that there was nondiscrimination in historical salary administration. These same employers report that they are unsure how they will proceed in the future, as they fear being audited via pay bands.

Other companies under federal investigation complied with data requests and provided salary information by broadband. When the investigator conducted macro analyses by bands and questioned why the minority group members' and/or women's median or average salaries were lower than others within these bands, the employers successfully articulated an "apples and oranges" defense. That is, *"You can't compare these by broadband as there are a variety of titles. They're too different."* Uncertain as to how to proceed in these cases, the investigators agreed to return these audits back to a title-by-title analysis. Was an analysis by title the most proper? Could the case have been made to audit these companies by band?

It remains uncertain whether these same employers *should* have been audited by the entire broadband, zones within the bands or other control points within the bands, or job title. What is certain is that while there may be a number of virtues to broadbanding, ensuring nondiscrimination will be a challenge. "Banding presumes that managers will manage employee pay to accomplish the organization's objectives (and not their own) and treat employees fairly …. The challenge today is to take advantage of flexibility without increasing labor costs or leaving the organization vulnerable to charges of favoritism or inconsistency."[39] Broadbanding "risks self-serving and potentially inequitable decisions on the part of the manager."[40]

As of yet, there does not appear to be overriding concern from America's corporate leadership regarding the implications that broadbanding may have upon their responsibilities to ensure nondiscrimination in the workplace. Is this because routine audits by the federal government to date revert quickly back to a title-by-title analysis? Do federal investigators realize that by reverting to a title-by-title analysis, they have lost the broad oversight and monitoring abilities brought by the salary grade approach?

Recent studies find no greater increase in discrimination claims by companies using broadbanding.[41] As with other employment issues, is it due to lack of knowledge?

To reinforce an earlier point, any compensation system bears the potential for bias and discrimination and should be monitored. Systems that give greater latitude and discretion to a manager may warrant closer attention.

Most importantly, review one's system proactively, well before an EEO charge or an OFCCP investigation.

Add to this already complex equation the fact that there is an emerging corporate trend toward rewarding employees with compensation components above base salary. Far too frequently, the real discrepancy isn't in base salary — it's in bonuses, stock options and the like. How should these components be reviewed? Who should get access to these data? How will rank-and-file field investigators review such data? These are all issues just beginning to emerge in the area of equal pay. Presently, few ask for this additional information and even fewer know what to do with it.

A Federal Example

In the past year, there has been much discussion about the need to reward federal employees for performance (merit pay) rather than tenure or time in grade. Broadbanding is one vehicle being discussed and, in some cases, used. This development raises an interesting question: "How will the federal government itself ensure nondiscrimination as it undertakes pilot projects in this arena?" Until now, the federal government has positioned itself as a role model, ensuring nondiscrimination in pay by virtue of very little discretion. (See Figure 10.)

This is the general scale, though there are different pay scales for executives, law enforcement, scientists, etc. Note that there are 15 grades with 10 incremental steps in each. How will these 15 salary grades compress? How many bands? What ranges?

With many federal departments and agencies petitioning the U.S. Congress to broadband their pay ranges, each in its own fashion, there is question as to how much latitude should be given to individual federal agencies and departments. An Office of Personnel Management (OPM) white paper on this subject states that the federal pay system is disintegrating. "Through special authorities, a number of agencies already have begun to move toward more modern systems, and our ability to promote common policies across the government where appropriate is diminishing.[42]

If a federal agency broadbanded the 15 salary grades into five bands, each band would be three traditional salary grades wide. (See Figure 11.)

Innumerable salary scenarios can unfold. For example, an entry-level investigator being hired traditionally at a GS-7 or $29,037-plus (depending upon variables such as prior experience and prior pay), could now be hired at ... what? Any salary within Band III? How much latitude does a manager

FIGURE 10: 2003 SALARY TABLE FOR FEDERAL GOVERNMENT EMPLOYEES-GS

Incorporating a 3.10% General Increase
Effective January 2003
Annual Rates by Grade and Step

GRADE	STEP 1	STEP 2	STEP 3	STEP 4	STEP 5	STEP 6	STEP 7	STEP 8	STEP 9	STEP 10
GS-1	$15,214	$15,722	$16,228	$16,731	$17,238	$17,536	$18,034	$18,538	$18,559	$19,031
GS-2	17,106	17,512	18,079	18,559	18,767	19,319	19,871	20,423	20,975	21,527
GS-3	18,664	19,286	19,908	20,530	21,152	21,774	22,396	23,018	23,640	24,262
GS-4	20,952	21,650	22,348	23,046	23,744	24,442	25,140	25,838	26,536	27,234
GS-5	23,442	24,223	25,004	25,785	26,566	27,347	28,128	28,909	29,690	30,471
GS-6	26,130	27,001	27,872	28,743	29,614	30,485	31,356	32,227	33,098	33,969
GS-7	29,037	30,005	30,973	31,941	32,909	33,877	34,845	35,813	36,781	37,749
GS-8	32,158	33,230	34,302	35,374	36,446	37,518	38,590	39,662	40,734	41,806
GS-9	35,519	36,703	37,887	39,071	40,255	41,439	42,623	43,807	44,991	46,175
GS-10	39,115	40,419	41,723	43,027	44,331	45,635	46,939	48,243	49,547	50,851
GS-11	42,976	44,409	45,842	47,275	48,708	50,141	51,574	53,007	54,440	55,873
GS-12	51,508	53,225	54,942	56,659	58,376	60,093	61,810	63,527	65,244	66,961
GS-13	61,251	63,293	65,335	67,377	69,419	71,461	73,503	75,545	77,587	79,629
GS-14	72,381	74,794	77,207	79,620	82,033	84,446	86,859	89,272	91,685	94,098
GS-15	85,140	87,978	90,816	93,654	96,492	99,330	102,168	105,006	107,844	110,682

have? Is there that much discretion? It most likely will vary by agency and department.

The small number of federal agencies currently moving toward broadbanding within their work forces may articulate that such bands must adhere to EEO and Merit Systems principles:

"Equal pay should be provided for work of equal value with appropriate consideration of both national and local rates paid by employers in the private sector, and appropriate incentives and recognition should be provided for excellence in performance."[43]

Ensuring such may prove more difficult. The OPM makes the case for a new, flexible compensation system for the federal work force to replace one that rewards longevity. While such modernization is important to attract and retain a quality federal work force, the federal government must be vigilant

FIGURE 11: NEW RANGES — THREE TRADITIONAL SALARY GRADES WIDE

Band I	$15,214	to	$24,262
Band II	$20,952	to	$33,969
Band III	$29,037	to	$46,175
Band IV	$39,115	to	$66,961
Band V	$61,251	to	$110,682

to ensure that its own system(s) are monitored to ensure nondiscrimination. How will fairness and pay equity be ensured at those government agencies moving toward a broadbanding environment complete with pay for performance? There is no "new money" or profits from which to pay for performance, leaving workers wondering what the source of funding shall be? Will standard cost-of-living increases (generally 2 percent to 3 percent of salary) be included in this cash pool and no longer a "given?" Will the U.S. government's enormous strides toward inclusion and fairness of the last 30 years be undone? What will happen to the esprit de corps? Will morale be affected when there is differentiation in pay for those doing the exact same task, or holding the exact same rank or title?

All such flexibility gained in philosophical and structural shifts needs to be accompanied by fairness; otherwise, government risks becoming "the pot calling the kettle black."

6

Team Efforts

T he use of teams or task forces to resolve a problem or advance a product has become quite common in America's workplaces. There are a variety of manners in which individuals convene in a team format … often bringing individuals from different offices, departments and divisions.

A team is "a group of people working together towards a common goal."[44] Teams often arise as a result of a business need. It is through this collaborative effort that better products, methodologies or services are produced. Teams often participate in exercises to improve their cohesiveness. There are many structural differences in teams. Teambuilding experts talk of high-performing work teams, self-managing work teams, problem-solving teams, quality circles, functional teams and cross-functional teams. While there are many methods of identifying team members, the teams that are most effective have common traits:

- Clear goals

- Good communication

- Unified commitment

- Mutual trust

- Effective leadership

- External and internal support

- Negotiating and relevant skills.[45]

The end result of each is a common goal. While there is enormous variability in team structure, there also is great variability in time commitment. There are full-time teams that are permanent, full-time teams that are short-term (coming together full-time to work on an issue) and part-time teams (in which individuals continue their full-time employment status but come together on a periodic basis). When teams are longer in duration, consultants and experts often are called upon to walk members through the stages of team building (forming, storming, norming and performing) in an effort to produce an open and trusting atmosphere where the common goal can be achieved. With such variability in time commitment, form and function, how can pay equity be ensured?

The first step is identifying a compensation plan. What type of pay plan should be adopted? The combinations are numerous: merit pay, skill-based pay, group incentives, gain sharing, pay tied to demonstration of competencies, peer evaluation within the team and nonmonetary awards (cups, mugs, etc.), to name a few. How does one choose between an individual plan and a group plan? (See Figure 12.)

How does one ensure pay equity in the scenario chosen? The simplest scenario is one in which all of the individuals report to the same manager. Regardless of the "type" of team, that manager should have some objective knowledge of individual and group production to compensate each of these team members in an equitable fashion. A singular manager can more readily ensure there is individual pay equity in a group setting than teams where there are multiple direct reports.

FIGURE 12: THE CHOICE BETWEEN INDIVIDUAL AND GROUP PLANS[46]		
Characteristic	**Choose an Individual Plan when ...**	**Choose a Group Plan when ...**
Performance Measurement	Good measures of individual performance exist. Task accomplishment not dependent on other's performance.	Output is group collaborative effort. Individual contributions to output cannot be assessed.
Organizational Adaptability	Individual performance standards are stable. Production methods and labor mix relatively constant.	Performance standards for individuals change to meet environmental pressures on relatively constant organizational objectives. Production methods and labor mix must adapt to meet changing pressures.
Organizational Commitment	Commitment strongest to individual's profession or superior. Supervisor viewed as unbiased and performance standards readily apparent.	High commitment to organization built upon sound communication or organizational objectives and performance standards.
Union Status	Nonunion. Unions promote equal treatment. Competition between individuals inhibits "fraternal" spirit.	Union or nonunion. Unions less opposed to plans that foster cohesiveness of bargaining unit and which distribute rewards evenly across group.

How should pay equity be ensured in situations where the team members report to different managers and lines of authority? While one manager may handsomely reward an employee who served on a team, the manager of another team member may not. Is this equitable?

Dialogue is an integral tool to ensuring pay equity in a team setting. There should be open communication between managers regarding the performance process and resultant rewards of the team and its members. Such dialogue should be ongoing to meet expectations to ensure large disparities do not exist. Large variations in the rewards of individual members may work against the cohesiveness of the team, especially when the group is ongoing over several performance review and pay cycles. While disparities may not be discriminatory, they can cause disharmony and break down the team's dynamics.

In other cases, teams come and go — often during a single performance cycle. Though this will make it difficult for the compensation professional to weigh in on ensuring equity and fairness, clear guidance should be promulgated for management to follow. This same oversight goes beyond base pay to the use of bonuses and stock options, two vehicles widely used in these situations. The issue warranting greater scrutiny in the team setting is that of great variations in team or task force member awards. Can they be justified? Are they documented?

7

Compensation Beyond Base Pay

W hile salary discrimination continues unabated today in some workplace settings, base salary is becoming a smaller and smaller percentage of many workers' financial packages. As difficult as it is for management to appropriately monitor base salary, imagine the impediments to reviewing every component of compensation within your company to ensure fairness.

Actual differential pay in the form of bonuses, incentive pay, commissions and profit sharing generally are not addressed during proactive routine audits by the federal government. While the federal investigators from the U.S. Department of Labor's OFCCP report they do ask questions about bonuses during the roughly 200 corporate management glass ceiling audits conducted each year, it is unclear how much access or what type of information they receive. Some of the most protracted audits have resulted from incomplete or conflicting information having been provided. What other variables in addition to merit increases affect base pay? What types of "bonus" programs does the company being reviewed offer and what data do these companies provide? Do they provide access to one type of program? One form of incentive pay? All?

The law enforcement situation is even bleaker in terms of investigators' knowledge base beyond salary. What does the average federal investigator know about stock options? Can that investigator be expected to value stock options vs. outright stock awards? What about the components of long-term incentive plans? Should an auditor be well versed in all of these components … a task that many in HR are trying to achieve? Add to this the enormous variability in benefits packages (e.g., variations in holiday leave, sick leave, disability packages, health care plans and insurance), and the level of corporate concern that there will be a thorough audit by the OFCCP drops sharply.

Should management be concerned? Why is there a need to self-audit compensation packages above base salary if there is no fear of an in-depth federal investigation? The reason management should feel compelled to do so, and do so today, is that self-auditing for potential pay inequities would help restore trust in America's workplaces. How important is it to review compensation above salary? How large is this other component of one's compensation? In 1999, salary, or base pay, accounted for only 41 percent of American workers' compensation. Long-term incentives were 27 percent, followed by bonuses and benefits at 14 percent, respectively. Perquisites represented only 4 percent of compensation in the U.S.[47] So, while investigators struggle to obtain access to salary data and audit for discrimination, for many, this is a shrinking piece of the pie.

In addition to understanding annual awards beyond base salary, knowing what to request and how to review and analyze it are important "next steps" in ensuring nondiscrimination in America's workplaces. For managers to be able to conduct such analyses proactively, intervention by senior management and cooperation between HR departments is required.

The Bonus

The use of the "bonus" has been around seemingly forever. In fields that are sales-driven, bonuses and commissions are integral components of compensation. In other employment areas, the bonus remains a one-off after the fact for a job well done, or as a gesture at the holidays. Who gets these, in what amounts and for what are important questions that management should ask. If such bonuses are tied to a specific project, a host of questions warrants asking, beginning with "Did anyone validate the sales quotas?" "Did everyone on the project receive a bonus award?" "Why is this person's award so much larger than that person's?" If tied to performance, the routine issues of validating that performance and ensuring equity arise.

In other settings, certain salary grades or positions are deemed bonus eligible. You may not know it, but you too may have a position that is eligible. You may not have ever received a bonus, but your peers may have. How many of us have ever thought to ask: "Is this position bonus eligible?" This means, is *anyone* at this position able to receive a bonus? By asking such questions, one becomes aware what *might* be available to oneself or one's peers. Similarly, by requesting the performance measures or competencies required to attain a bonus, one may be able to benefit more fully from the bonus pool of monies in the future. The challenge is to effectively audit proactively for problem areas.

Some of the methods for performing a proactive audit outside an investigation include:

- Systemic review of bonuses person-by-person using the title-by-title matrix approach

- Systemic review using average or median bonus paid

- Systemic review using average or median bonus as a percentage of pay

- A demographic review of those "left behind" ... bonus eligible but not receiving.

Did this latter group have equal or better performance yet receive no additional award? Had it served on the same task force, yet no award?

Since a good federal investigator would do the same, an annual review is warranted.

Referral Bonus

Employers use many types of bonuses. One such vehicle is widely used by employers having a difficult time attracting talent — the referral bonus. This is not an annual bonus, but is relatively common. Fifty-nine percent of companies responding to a 2002 referral survey report that their organization has a referral bonus program in place. The average bonus awarded ranged from $1,000-$2,499 at the majority of companies.[48] An annual review of this system would include:

- What referrals were accepted?

- Were the referrals that were accepted predominantly from one demographic group?

- Is anyone ensuring that this means of acquiring new talent (and rewarding current employees) is nondiscriminatory?

- Is anyone monitoring the bonus variability to ensure equity?

Sign-on Bonus

A December 2001 survey revealed the broad use of sign-on bonuses as a form of compensation other than base pay. For purposes of this survey, it is important to clarify that companies with a program do not necessarily use the cash bonus in all cases, but all categories are eligible for the program. The following are some survey highlights:

- Sixty-two percent of the surveyed companies had a sign-on bonus, and 17 percent of those have a program that includes all positions.

- Seventy-seven percent said this program was helping the company attract new talent, down from 88 percent in 2000.

- A majority of participants have had no changes to their use of sign-on bonuses in the past 12 months (average of 62 percent).

- In most cases (86.5 percent), this bonus was a flat dollar amount.

- For the executive rank, 86 percent of the companies have the bonus and this remains the norm, increasing from 83 percent in 2000.

The amounts were often quite substantial with 83 percent stating that bonuses were greater than $10,000 for executives (42 percent of whom receive bonuses of more than $25,000), 55 percent stating that bonuses were greater than $10,000 for senior management, 72 percent stating that bonuses were greater than $5,000 for middle management, and about 60 percent stating the bonuses were between $1,000 and 5,000 for supervisors, professional staff and technical staff.[49]

One company self-auditing its compensation system found that women were being paid less at time of hire than men. When the layers were peeled away, it became apparent that men were being granted sign-on bonuses that became institutionalized into base salary. The argument was that these were necessary to attract this talent base. Senior management ceased the practice of granting sign-on bonuses. The results were dramatic: an assurance of pay equity at time of hire, and no drop off in the quantity or quality of the new talent hired.

Retention Bonus

For other companies, the need to use cash incentives to retain employees can obviously become paramount when, as was the case in the late 1990s, the labor market is extremely tight and employers get into bidding wars to lure the employees of competitors. But retention bonuses are not just useful and necessary in tight labor markets. Indeed, when economic conditions soften and companies begin to struggle or face reorganization, retaining key employees can mean the difference between success and failure.

It was in the latter environment, in mid-2002, that WorldatWork re-fielded a Retention Bonus Survey instrument that had previously been fielded to members in the very tight, March 2000, labor market.

Interestingly, the 2002 survey data indicates a slightly higher prevalence of retention bonus in the more difficult market conditions. In 2000, about 24 percent of the 650 WorldatWork members who responded to the survey reported having a retention bonus program in place. In May 2002, however, 34 percent of the 772 members indicated their organization has a retention bonus program.

The different economic environments of 2000 and 2002 might explain the difference in payment practices of retention awards. In 2000, 75 percent of respondents said that payments were made as lump sums, but in 2002 that figure was reduced to 65 percent, perhaps reflecting the need in 2000 to put cash in people's pockets quickly to get them to not think about another offer, versus the need in 2002 to give cash at an interval or on a time schedule.

When asked in the May 2002 survey about the primary goal of the retention bonus program, the highest response (25 percent) indicated the bonuses were used to "retain key employees during organizational restructure." The second most common response, at 18 percent, was to "ensure long-term organizational continuity." Finally, in response to the question of whether the retention bonus program is an effective tool in retaining top talent, 84 percent of respondents in 2002 indicated in the affirmative.[50]

Is anyone at your company auditing the use of retention bonuses to ensure they are equitable?

Spot Bonus

More than half the companies responding to a 2002 WorldatWork survey stated they had a spot bonus program. This was primarily used for "above and beyond" behavior and special recognition. Those that utilize such a program report that it is an effective tool in retaining talent.[51] The use of this "pat on the back" bonus often continues even if a company is experiencing an economic downturn.

Whatever the type of bonus, whether it be a one-off or an ongoing payout, an internal review is vital to ensure fairness. The systems developed are most likely neutral, but ensuring the administration of each cash component is neutral should be an integral component of any bonus system. A simple data run could produce a matrix of each form of bonus, coupled with employee identifier, race/gender, reason for bonus and bonus amount. This then should be reviewed for internal equity under the auspices of attorney-client privilege and attorney-client work product.

Total Cash Compensation

As mentioned earlier, many companies have embarked on a "pay for performance" strategy that allows greater differential in pay in the form of a bonus. This bonus, coupled with base salary increases, forms a total cash pool that individuals manage. While there may be a cap on annual salary increases in this setting (i.e., three percent to five percent of base salary), there may not be tight fiscal controls on the bonus component. This may be the area with the greatest latitude warranting oversight. Just as managers receive extensive instructions how to manage this cash pool, they also should receive extensive instructions on how to ensure fairness within this system.

Managers should be cautioned that even in a total cash scenario where base salary increases are marginal, base salaries still should be audited in isolation for equity. I recently asked a federal investigator:

"If I brought you a company that's using a total cash pool approach (base and bonus combined) and was proactively monitoring such for nondiscrimination, would you allow it to show this information during audits, rather than base salary alone?"

The investigator's response was: *"No. I'll tell you why. Base salary is the only thing that is a 'given.' There is latitude in the bonus, and I still have to ensure that the floor is level."*

Therefore, it is recommended that the base salary component, the bonus component and the resultant total cash compensation amount be reviewed in isolation in a systemic fashion to ensure equity.

Stock Options

Remaining competitive always has been a challenge, but it has become an even greater challenge for America's businesses of late. A survey of 750 North American companies across major industries found that "companies most likely to compete for talent on the basis of salary alone are those with relatively lower performance."[52]

> "I didn't even know there were stock options available at my level. Then, last year, I got some as a result of my performance review. Who knew?"
>
> — *Entry-level manager*

The use of stock options has skyrocketed in the past decade in response to this challenge. In some industries, the use of stock options has allowed the company to stay competitive while rewarding key performers."... [S]tock option use among ... organizations is unavoidable if a company is committed to remaining competitive. The distribution of equity via stock options has become a key factor in the overall business strategy of most high-tech firms. And options are making a strong case for themselves as value-delivery vehicles."[53]

To those with no experience with this form of compensation, the stock option remains a mystery. In simple terms it is a right to purchase a fixed number of shares of the company at a fixed price over a specified time period after certain time requirements are met. Specifically, one may receive a performance award in the form of "X stock options" at the price of $Y after Z number of years. Obviously, the employee would only exercise this right, or purchase these shares of stock, at a future date *if* the stock price was higher. Thus, this is an inducement for employees to work to ensure that the company remains competitive so that the stock price rises. There are qualified incentive stock options and nonqualified stock options (See definitions.)

Definitions

A qualified incentive stock option qualifies for favorable tax treatment in that there is no tax at exercise and long-term capital gains treatment if shares are held for one year after exercise and two years after grant before sale. The company may not deduct it as a business expense.

A nonqualified stock option does not qualify for special tax treatment under Section 422 of the Internal Revenue Code. The excess over fair market value is taxed as ordinary income. The company may deduct it as a business expense.

Qualified stock options help in retention and motivation of key employees and are not offered to all. While there are differences between these two vehicles, qualified stock options can have the more favorable tax treatment — there is no tax at the time the option is granted and they are taxed as long-term capital gains (only about 20 percent) if one buys and sells the stock within a certain time period.[54]

Historically, exercising stock options brought trade-offs for the employee. In the past, an order to turn such options into actual shares required a large outlay of cash. With the birth of the "cashless exercising of stock options comma," an employee can exercise the option and simultaneously sell it without having to come up with the cash up front. "Now with the use of cashless exercising of these options, it makes them a much more attractive part of an employee compensation package."[55] The employee also may use a stock swap to exercise this option. That is, the employee would use stock already owned to "swap" and exercise the option.

Stock options should not be confused with stock purchase plans in which employees can purchase shares of the company's stock, usually at a lower than market price and/or with the company's contribution to such. The former are outright awards that can only be used at a later date. The latter are an opportunity for an employee to become a shareholder in its employer at a reduced rate.

While the stock option may have been limited to a relative few individuals in the past, the marked increase in their use, especially in high-tech and fast-growing industries, has been widely documented. And, while there has been much ballyhoo regarding the decline in net worth of those whose stock has plummeted, the stock option continues to be a vital compensation tool.

Those companies that saw their wealth dry up with the decline in stock prices in the last few years now debate such measures as reducing the exercise price of existing options, canceling existing options and issuing new ones with a lower exercise price, and/or issuing new options and allowing the worthless options to expire unexercised. Employers debate the consequences of each of these alternatives and the effect any of these will have on previously granted options. However, a Hewitt survey of 202 major employers found that 52 percent of companies will maintain the current proportion of stock used in its compensation portfolio. Forty-two percent of the companies are planning greater educational efforts on the risks and rewards of company stock.[56] This is mirrored by a WorldatWork member survey that found that employer's efforts to use stock options for motivational and retention purposes were undercut by employees' ignorance as to how they work. Compounding the trauma of the falling value of the stock itself is the push to have stock options expensed — whether by force or as a proactive measure. How this will play out is anyone's guess. But, many still say the stock option is here to stay.

For those hit hard by falling stock prices, the stock option may have become a less viable retention tool. These companies have had to explore a myriad of other devices including a repricing of the stock options that have bottomed out. For others, the very real fear that options and employee stock-purchase plans will be subject to Social Security, Medicare and unemployment taxes in the offing make them less ideal, as well. In some instances companies are turning to compensation vehicles typically restricted to executives to retain key performers during these tough times.

The bottom line is:

- At what employment levels are individuals eligible to receive options?

- Who has been granted options, and how many?

- Is there documentation of the performance that led to each grant?

- Upon review, did other people in the same situation not receive options?

- What is the demographic composition of those who received vs. those who were "similarly situated" (i.e., could have received)?

- Is there anyone who reviews this compensation component to ensure fairness?

Executive Compensation

> "We had an executive who just left the company after two years. He wasn't even with us the full five years for his stock to vest. He walked away from a bundle."
>
> — *Employee unaware of the executive's shorter vesting restrictions*

Unlike the stock option that is now widely used throughout many workplaces, several long-term incentive awards are administered solely at the executive level. While many long-term incentives are available, the following are some of the most popular:

- **Phantom stock plans** — cash or stock awarded to an executive based upon the increase in the company's stock price at a fixed future date

- **Stock appreciation rights** — cash or stock awards that are determined by the increase in the company's stock price during any given time chosen by the executive in the option period.

Neither of these incentive packages requires any financing by the executive. Another retention tool used by many companies of late is the stock grant.

- **Stock grant plans** provide stock to employees without them incurring any cost. The stock grants may entitle the employee the appreciated value of the stock over a designated period of time (stock-appreciation grants) or may be an outright grant to the employee of the total value of the stock over a predetermined period (full-value grant).

- **Restricted stock plans** grant stock at a reduced price to the executive with the condition that it may not be sold before a specific date (usually four to five years). The executive receives the dividends, but must forfeit the stock if he/she terminates before the restriction period ends.

While stock options have received a great deal of negative attention of late, due largely to some specific corporations and their stock, these are important issues to understand and navigate.

The use of stock as a strong tool in the compensation equation — even if cash compensation remains the same or drops due to business trends — is not a small-ticket item. There has been a marked increase in the use of options in the past 10 years. While one million U.S. employees were eligible for them a decade ago, that number increased to 7 million by 2000, according to the National Center for Employee Ownership.

While the federal government expanded its mandate theoretically in these areas with its corporate management (glass ceiling) reviews, it has yet to fully explore any of these issues. Relatively few, if any, of those charged with the legal enforcement of nondiscrimination laws have had enough exposure to review these types of rewards packages. With the variability in the vehicles and their terms (vested or not vested, fair market value, forfeiture of stock, forced sale of stock, etc.), thorough analysis may prove difficult. Add to this equation the fact that the compensation professionals who administer these programs may not be the same individuals who conduct salary administration, and the circle of individuals required to ensure fairness gets even wider.

Ensuring fairness *above* base salary is uncharted waters for many in HR and federal investigators alike. But, as it becomes a larger share of the total rewards equation, it will not remain so.

8

Circling Back to Performance

"My husband just received the highest rating possible at his law firm. Yet, he received no pay increase or annual bonus. What do you think this means? Do you think the firm is doing poorly? Or, could the firm be giving him a positive performance evaluation before they let him go?"

— *Lawyer's spouse*

While much of this book has been dedicated to how people are paid and the variability in rewards structures, performance, almost universally, is the key driving force in how individuals are rewarded by their employers. Any group of individuals holding the exact same title may have differing salaries based upon a number of variables that came into play over the course of their work lives. While there is a myriad of such variables, performance tends to have the strongest link to salary.

Small employers may not use a formal written performance evaluation system. Conversations may take the place of written assessments and cyclical feedback. Salary increases and bonuses may be the result of verbal discussions and salary negotiations, with very few formal records retained.

In large work forces, there are two general performance evaluation formats — ranking and rating. Employees are compared and ordered in some form of rank or order in ranking formats. This can be done by straight, alternating or paired comparisons. In rating formats, employees are actually given a numerical score(s) for individual performance, and not compared to others.[57]

A large company may use one or both of these formats, each at various times during the compensation cycle(s). A company may use ratings for actual performance coupled with needs assessments for salary increases. This might be performed at the end of the fiscal year. This same company might utilize rankings for determining bonuses and other awards at the end of the calendar year. A company may require a manager to ensure that all ratings fit neatly into a bell-shaped curve (1-5 or 1-7) with very few ones and fives (or sevens) and the bulk of employees in the middle range. Or a company's philosophy may be that a rating below a certain level signifies a poor performer, one who's ready "for the door." There even can be great variability within a company concerning how these systems are administered. One manager may give no "1"s at all; another may give a healthy sprinkling. How is it possible to review such practices to ensure fairness?

Add to this quagmire the fact that other assessment formats including narrative-based "write-ups" and management by objectives may never make it into a database at all. In fact, several types being used at any one employer's workplace may be dependent upon division or even manager. This is a nightmare for the HR professional wanting to proactively ensure equity in his or her division or business unit.

With the competing demands managers face today, sitting down and documenting the performance of one's subordinates appear to rank toward the bottom. It is much more important (and easier) to give the rating, ranking or award percentage, and skim over the documentation in a cursory fashion. Yet, capturing and documenting performance are make-it or break-it points for many companies. A performance evaluation needs to stand on its own to be credible. A formal assessment is often the decision point for promotions, as well as displacements. When promotions are called into question or appealed, all eyes turn toward the documentation. Likewise, when companies realign, they feel the heat for evaluations that were insufficient in documentation or completion. Shouldn't there be the same importance placed upon performance evaluations on an ongoing basis?

A cursory evaluation may leave the employee uncertain of how well he or she is doing, as well as unaware of areas warranting improvement. It may leave the employee believing he or she is doing well, when that person actually is going to be let go. A good evaluation may not necessarily lead to an above-average salary increase or bonus, either.

Annual assessments raise a unique set of concerns. An annual assessment may bring to light issues that may not have ever been discussed during the assessment cycle. Without periodic feedback during the year, an employee may be in a state of shock to learn of developmental weaknesses at the annual assessment. Such assessments have always been prone to many forms of bias, as well. These range from the "halo error" in which an appraiser gives a positive rating on all aspects of performance due to one job function being performed in a superior fashion to the "horn error" which is the opposite — when an appraiser marks an employee lower on all aspects because one job function was done poorly. There is also the "clone error" in which employees who are like the rater in behavior or personality are rated higher and the "spillover error" in which an employee is consistently downgraded because of performance errors during prior rating cycles. There are a host of other types of bias focusing on first impressions and tendencies to generally rate low or high.[58]

For companies attempting to circumvent bias and provide more employee guidance, the birth of 360-degree feedback as a means of assessment was welcomed. (See Figure 13.) 360-degree feedback is a formal process of assessment by one's subordinate(s), peer(s), manager(s) and customer(s).

This type of assessment has helped alleviate manager/ rater bias because it receives input from management, several customers, several peers and several subordinates. The format also has been credited with

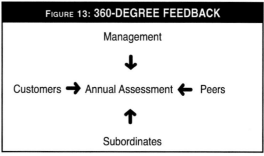

FIGURE 13: 360-DEGREE FEEDBACK

Management

↓

Customers → Annual Assessment ← Peers

↑

Subordinates

improving behaviors and recognizing customer satisfaction and performance that may have been previously overlooked. For some employers, however, this process — which was once welcomed — has now become much too labor intensive and burdensome. Some who find virtue in this type of assessment have reduced or streamlined the process to only one subordinate, one or two peers and customers to alleviate this time constraint.

What is being assessed varies from workplace to workplace. Assessments may not be solely performance-based. One company might use a knowledge-based pay system in which salary differentiation is based upon specialized training, formal educational attainment or specific field. At another company, assessments might be based on current performance alone, while at the next employer it might be current performance as well as leadership potential.

It bears noting at this juncture that subjective issues such as "potential" and "leadership" are often called into question. Just as there is the saying "Always the bridesmaid never the bride," many members of minority groups and women claim that while they are placed into higher-level leadership positions on an "acting" basis, a Caucasian or male often fills the position. Subjective criteria warrant greater oversight and documentation.

More recently, many companies have embraced competency-based performance systems that reward those behaviors that companies value. While these types of assessments have been in existence for decades for developmental purposes, it is only in the recent past that such have been used to reward performance. Companies using such systems have stated that these systems have raised overall performance, changed behaviors and even altered the measure of success at the company. How these systems marry up with compensation determinations varies with each company. Some reward competency attainment, others competency growth. If an individual is found to be below the target level, he/she may get below the target rate in compensation. Some companies may take a person-based approach to competency-based pay, others, a role-based approach.

Performance Reviews

Almost everyone dreads performance review time. Managers with time constraints dread having to set aside time to formally document employee performance. Employees dread it as well. Even if a manager provides "continual feedback" to his/her employees, the annual documentation of performance and "the discussion" are cause for anxiety. Couple this with the fact that employees don't like assessments either: Sixty-five percent of those who responded to a TrueCareers survey said they were dissatisfied with their most recent salary review.[59] Whatever the approach, ensuring that performance is accurately documented is vital.

During the course of an investigation, if an auditor finds that minorities or women are disproportionately terminated, they will review personnel files and termination papers. A good investigator then will interview and inquire to ensure that there was not disparate treatment of these individuals.

While such a review *should* be proactively conducted to ensure nondiscrimination, many companies have found they have insufficient performance documentation when faced with having to downsize, realign or rightsize. "How can we displace those who have been performing poorly if we didn't document it?" was the cry at many companies. In some cases, while formal assessments should have been taking place on a routine basis because they are the foundation for promotions, salary increases and other forms of remuneration, it is only when realigning the work force that documentation was found to be inadequate, sloppy or nonexistent. Ensuring proper documentation is just as important on the way up the ladder as on the way down.

During a review of rankings, a female employee's "glowing" written assessment did not seem to marry-up to her ranking. Upon questioning, the manager remarked that she was happy with her assessment, got a merit increase and seemed pleased. When questioned whether this mirrored her performance, he stated that giving her actual performance feedback would have made her cry. Meanwhile, this employee did not know she had deficiencies. Likewise, she was not aware that there was a "closed" or secret ranking process used by management.

Artificial assessments do no one any good. Closed performance systems warrant debate as well. *The Knowledge of Pay Study* (WorldatWork, 2002) claims that corporate turnover and poor performance issues are linked with traditional closed performance and compensation systems.[60] So, why the secrecy? Why not make systems more transparent? What should an employer do to ensure nondiscrimination?

In general terms, a performance appraisal system should:

- Give specific written instructions on how to complete the appraisal.

- Incorporate clear criteria on how to evaluate performance.

- Adequately develop job descriptions.

- Make it clear how different components of the evaluation are weighted. Work to assure that the factors are applied consistently for all employees.

- Evaluate honestly. Overly inflated assessments can lead to discrimination claims and employee morale issues.

- Require supervisors to provide feedback about appraisal results to affected employees.

- Incorporate a review by a higher-level official.

- Contain consistency across raters to ensure nondiscrimination with regard to race, color, religion, sex and national origin.[61]

- Document well. Examples of exceptional work or poor work should be maintained with the performance assessment.

Systemic Assessment

An annual review of performance ratings and rankings is critical to ensuring nondiscrimination. Whether it is the desire for a bell-shaped curve, a proportional approach or a forced ranking system, a review systemwide will ensure the playing field is level. Such a review ought to be conducted under the auspices of attorney-client privilege. Just as in compensation analyses, if there are trends that warrant closer analysis, a "spot-check" of the actual assessments to ensure that they mirror such ratings and rankings is recommended. Just as there have always been teachers who are hard graders, there may be managers who are exceptionally hard — or lenient — on their employees' ratings. Is the corporate performance management system uniformly applied? For example:

- If a "new to grade" is to receive a "3" rating the first cycle, is this being done uniformly? Or, could a "new to grade" receive a 2 or a 4?

- Is there is a clustering of minority group members or women at the low end of the rating or ranking system?

- Is this clustering of minority group members or women isolated to a particular salary grade? A division?

In many instances, a review of personnel files may be warranted. It could be that these individuals are not performing well and a closer review of the workplace setting is warranted. Or, it could be that these individuals are high-fliers, moving through the system quickly, and therefore skewed to the lower end of the curve because they are "new to grade." Without peeling away the layers to identify the root cause, one would only be theorizing.

9

Good Employers

P ublications abound with "model employers." Almost every publication and periodical tailored to minority group members and/or women have an entire issue dedicated to good employers. Many of these employers are enlightened and provide a workplace that is not only worker friendly, but also may have policies catering to the specific needs of their employees. While most employers offer standard pensions, hospitalization, life insurance, sick/annual leave, vacation leave, maternity leave and even adoption leave, other employers are leading the charge to create a workplace that helps employees manage the competing demands of their lives. Some of these benefits include:

- Before- and after-school care programs
- Catastrophic leave assistance
- Childcare for sick children
- Childcare and/or forums
- Christmas/Holiday bonus
- College scholarships for dependents
- Compressed work schedules
- Contributions to thrift plans
- Discount on goods
- Education expenditures
- Eldercare seminars
- Emergency back-up childcare
- Employee assistance programs
- Employee meals (furnished or subsidized by the company)
- Flex-time
- Flex-place
- Health programs

- Job sharing
- Lactation rooms
- Life insurance, death benefits and/or dental insurance
- On-site dry cleaning
- On-site recreation and athletic facilities
- On-site store/pharmacy
- Parenting resource centers
- Part-time employment
- Profit sharing.

These benefits should not be taken lightly as they do have a cost to the employer and can be large cost items in one's total rewards package. Whether the employer truly *is* family-friendly is another question.

"While businesses may have good intentions when they start family-friendly initiatives, they're also looking for 'good P.R.' .... Often, there's a strong informal message that you aren't supposed to use them," claims Joan Williams, director of the program on gender, work and family at American University's law school.[62]

This may be the case that some employers or managers discourage the participation in flexible work-family programs. Or, while many benefits may be offered, it may be that employees want to stay at work and only use those benefits that make doing so easier (e.g., on-site daycare, dry cleaning, reduced-cost take-out dinners).

Author Arlie Russell Hochschild, in her book, *TimeBind*, offers the theory that workers may feel more appreciated and more competent at work than at home, and that work may feel like home and home may feel like work.[63] Regardless of the motives, many boast about and use the family friendly policies of America's workplaces.

At the executive level, the list of additional benefits is exhaustive — with each executive negotiating a "personal" package. This list could include use of the company jet or flying first class; apartments in major U.S. cities; private school reimbursements for children; and exclusive luncheon clubs and country club memberships.

Are any of these benefits more valuable than being paid properly? Does the laundry list of benefits offered by an employer have any correlation to an employer that pays its employees fairly? Some studies have shown that management cannot substitute additional benefits (or initiatives to make employees happy) for those rewards linked to performance. Money motivates. "The argument that money doesn't motivate simply collapses under the weight of research evidence ...." The vast majority of motivation researchers agree that money motivates.[64] Thus, being a good employer cannot be based on employment benefits alone. No matter what awards a company receives from interest groups, magazines or trade journals for its worker-friendly workplace, rewarding one's employees in a nondiscriminatory fashion should warrant the highest of accolades.

While trade publications have produced annual "good employer" lists for years, the federal government itself developed a positive "carrot" approach to enforcement in the late 1980s to balance out the big stick of enforcement it wields. Similar to the "good employer" awards bestowed by trade groups and magazines, the federal government began highlighting employers who are trying to be "model." At the U.S. Department of Labor these awards are the Secretary of Labor's Opportunity 2000 Award, the Exemplary Voluntary Efforts (EVE) Awards and the Exemplary Public Interest Contribution (EPIC) Award. Taken together these awards give recognition to dozens of companies trying to do the right thing ... beyond the letter of the law.

Throughout the years, there has been a marked increase in the creativity being shown by many employers — companies have expanded their recruitment efforts from the basic EEO/AA nondiscrimination tagline in employment advertisements to genuine relationships and partnerships with historically Black colleges and universities, as well as internships and mentoring. The majority of these efforts are in the recruitment and hiring arenas.

Best Compensation Practices

What does the Department of Labor's Office of Federal Contract Compliance recommend as "Best Compensation Practices?" The OFCCP advocates the following steps:

- The first step for an employer that is concerned about paying its workers fairly is a self-audit.

- Step two is to correct any problem areas identified by the self-audit.

- Step three is to create a set of procedures and practices for ensuring that all decisions on compensation in the future are based on job-related criteria that are consistent with business necessity and are applied uniformly and consistently to each and every pay decision.

Some of the best practices cited in this publication include:

- Conduct a job evaluation survey for each job in the facility to establish what the labor market in your area is paying for these occupations. Employers may choose to use "benchmark" positions for the sake of efficiency and economy.

- Train each individual who makes starting salary decisions in how to apply the company policy to starting salaries.[65]

The EEOC publication, "Best Practices for Private Sector Employers," a by-product of a public/private sector task force, mirrors these sentiments in its advice to be proactive. The EEOC task force recommends private sector employers:

- Monitor compensation practices and performance appraisal systems for discrimination.

- Ensure that employee compensation is linked to performance and skills.

- Establish and enforce an anti-discrimination policy.

- Eliminate practices which exclude or present barriers to minorities, women, persons with disabilities, older persons or any individual

- Link management pay to the contributions they make to ensuring a "discrimination free" work environment.[66]

The Chicago Area Partnerships (CAPS), an umbrella organization for community, government and corporate representatives in the Chicago area, developed and published its own "best practices" in 1996. In the area of compensation, the organization recommends: "Monitor all compensation practices and all elements of total compensation and appraisal systems for discrimination. Periodically review and evaluate factors critical to success."[67]

Are companies doing the right thing in silence? Sure. While there are a growing number of companies proactively reviewing compensation, many are timid about raising their hand. For example, Indianapolis-based Eli Lilly and Co. has publicized its three-step process: a) a median analysis similar to the OFCCP's; b) an analysis of payroll for deviations between men/women, minority group members and Caucasians; and c) a complex regression analysis utilizing tenure and performance. "You have to understand your own compensation system; then you have to figure in all the factors that affect that system," reports Greg Apple, manager of affirmative action programs.[68]

Proactive Salary Adjustments

One afternoon an employer called and said: *"At one of your speaking engagements on employment laws and compensation you discussed reviewing compensation decisions to ensure nondiscrimination. If I heard you right, if I have a female employee below the salary range and I have no firm reason why she would be the only one in such a situation I should ...."* The conversation went on for approximately 20 minutes with the executive providing me almost two dozen scenarios in which he could find no business reason that minority group members or women were being compensated below others. At the conclusion of the conversation, two dozen individuals had salary adjustments proactively ... by the employer. Yes, there are good employers that, when they know their legal responsibilities, will do the right thing ... albeit quietly. Are there enough of them? Not yet. Will you be one of them?

10

Formalizing Pay Equity

Very few people would argue that we should not enforce equal pay laws in the United States. If asked, the majority of employers would say they believe in the principles of fairness and nondiscrimination … though they may disagree on how to implement them. Even some of our most conservative organizations believe nondiscrimination mandates should be enforced. Though there is still discussion and debate as to how this should be conducted, ensuring pay equity should be a given.

How can we get there? How can we as a nation work together to ensure that no one is left behind due to bias or neglect? The solution begins at the top. Just as CEOs are credited with turning a business around or taking a company to new heights, the same should be said about pay equity.

Executive Leadership

Financial fairness necessitates executive leadership and senior management buy-in, just like any initiative, business shift or cultural change. If a company's executives want oversight and validation of the financial rewards employees receive, it will happen. One thing that CEOs understand is solid data analysis. While the principles of fairness resonate and are fodder for vignettes and anecdotes, when one "makes the case" that pay equity is of concern based upon sound internal legal and analytic review, executives respond. While the day-to-day management ought to be delegated, history has shown that all such efforts flourish with executive leadership. While compliance with the myriad of U.S. labor laws may make one grimace, it can be effortless if given executive backing and proper delegation. Ensuring that there is good corporate governance begins and ends with executive stewardship.

Coordinated Compensation Committee

While pay equity in compensation should begin with senior management, it is only through integrating the principles of equity throughout the work force that excellence will occur. "High-performing companies excel at the tough stuff — differentiating rewards for top performers and investing time in performance management and pay communications," claims a Towers Perrin study. Such companies "market and deliver rewards to employees on a more holistic and integrated basis."[69]

At many companies, each component of employee compensation, benefits and performance management may have a specific individual(s) who develop(s), monitor(s) and implement(s) that system. For example, there may be one person whose sole responsibility is ensuring that the company's salaries are similar to those of peers and competitors (external and internal equity studies). Another compensation specialist may only handle the bonus component and its rating process. There may be yet others who handle the paperwork and processing of executive level compensation. At another company, salary and bonus may be integrated and handled by one person or team, while at smaller companies all of these components may be handled by one or two people alone.

Without question, all professionals develop systems that they believe to be fair and unbiased. More often than not, these individuals have no oversight responsibilities to ensure that discrimination does not ensue. Yet these are the very best people to identify weaknesses in the system and where there is "play." It is for this reason that during federal audits and investigations, corporate compensation officials often will be interviewed. It is through the posing of theoretical situations that an investigator is able to identify areas warranting investigation and weaknesses warranting attention. It also is a way of validating the statements and facts that the EEO officer already has transmitted. If the compensation division has a working knowledge and understanding of nondiscrimination, coupled with the EEO officer's day-to-day administration of such, an audit should run more smoothly and be less protracted.

Using a coordinated compensation approach, appropriate individuals knowledgeable of wage and hour laws, EEO and nondiscrimination mandates and corporate compensation should be identified. Under the auspices of attorney-client privilege, this team should develop a methodology for monitoring compensation on routine basis. It is advisable that the analyses mentioned earlier be conducted as a baseline. Company-specific analyses should supplement this. If possible, such analyses should be conducted prior to the actual issuing of performance awards, bonuses or other forms of remuneration using "recommended awards" so that issues warranting further examination are identified early.

This team approach ought not dampen the flexibility managers need to reward top performers; rather, the team should work to ensure that any marked differences in compensation on a systemwide basis are highlighted. Those areas, business units, functions or divisions with marked differences should be responsible for ensuring that the performance that led to compensation differentiation is valid and documented. Just as companies "need to integrate pay design and delivery into a broader total rewards framework that reinforces the behavior and actions required of employees,"[70] so must nondiscrimination be woven into that fabric. Stronger oversight and systemic monitoring is warranted for the company embarking upon or using pay banding.

Competitive Compensation

Compensation professionals are some of the most trained HR employees a company can have. These employees readily discuss and debate trends occurring in their field, attend conferences and seminars and keep their credentials up-to-date. Ensuring that salaries remain competitive is a long-standing, never-ending task. Ensuring that the rewards the company offers are flexible and meet employee needs is an ongoing challenge. To remain competitive, an employer must ensure that its total rewards package meets the needs of today's and tomorrow's employees. The clarion call for compensation professionals is to make sure the playing field is level for all.

Complementary Diversity Efforts

For management to be successful, it needs to know what is expected. The battle for fairness will be lost if managers are caught in the quagmire of diversity bands and goals, salary grades, compensation bands and affirmative action goals. It is recommended that all corporate diversity efforts supplement the legal requirements already in place. Any additional workload and goal monitoring that is burdensome and conflicts with the legal requirements for nondiscrimination will not clear the waters; it will further muddy them.

Corporate Board Representation

Most major U.S. businesses have a corporate compensation committee made up of members of its board of directors. The corporate compensation committee at major employers serves in a number of vital roles and capacities to which nondiscrimination should be integral. Specifically, this body:

- Approves employment agreements with top executives, as well as compensation plans and pay levels for the CEO and other officers, taking into account similar practices outside the company

- Helps develop the guidelines for a pay-for-performance philosophy

- Ensures that executive succession planning and executive performance assessment mechanisms are in place
- Responds to stockholders' concerns regarding compensation and stock value
- Assists in the decision-making and management of the various compensation plans, such as stock options
- Communicates and performs a liaison activity with the board of directors, top management and federal government officials
- Reviews the impact the compensation plan would have in the event of a merger, acquisition or sale
- Produces the annual report on the committee's work.[71]

This component of the corporate board has received great scrutiny of late due to fiduciary concerns of employees and shareholders alike. While most publicity has surrounded CEO compensation, shareholder prices and stock-based retirement plans, ensuring the pay equity of the rank-and-file employee should be just as great a concern.

In fact, the coordinated compensation committee discussed earlier ought to report its results directly to this committee of the board. The role of human resources and corporate compensation undoubtedly will expand in this new era of scrutiny. "[B]est practices and competitive industry standards have become an insufficient basis for compensation committee decision-making ... In this new world of corporate governance, compensation committees will rely more on company compensation and HR professionals ...."

What does good governance look like? Jane T. Romweber of Hewitt Associates offers four specific items from the compensation committee's perspective[72]:

- Avoidance of excessive pay and extreme design practices
- Programs that promote good performance for shareholders and good business practices
- Actual payouts that relate to actual performance
- Program designs that are the product of due deliberation, with the shareholder always represented.

While some predict that the recent spate of corporate scandals may make it more difficult to find directors for corporate boards, it only can be seen as beneficial in acquiring such if a company clearly articulates its desire to ensure financial fairness within its work force. Ensuring that systems are in place to monitor for such equity within all components of remuneration will greatly assist in meeting the demand for good corporate governance.[73]

Communication

Communication is key. Research supports the need for clear, concise communication in almost every field. Human resources, and specifically compensation, is no different. High-performing companies have been found more likely to:

- Measure managers' ability to communicate about pay

- Measure the success of communication about the rewards structure

- Communicate the value of their total rewards — compensation, benefits and the work experience — to employees.[74]

If this is the case, why is there still secrecy about compensation and other forms of remuneration? Why do closed performance management systems exist? Executives, management and employees alike should be knowledgeable of the compensation strategy in place and the business imperative. Regardless of the performance system being used, clear communication surrounding performance and the rewards structure should alter and reinforce employee behavior. A strong link must not only exist but be reinforced. Serious consideration should be given to elimination of the taboos of compensation dialogues. A fair system is much easier to communicate than one steeped in vagueness. A proactive approach to pay equity should help provide assurances to stockholders of corporate integrity and accountability.

Endnotes and
Selected References

Endnotes

1   *Workforce 2000, Work and Workers for the 21st Century*, Executive Summary, The Hudson Institute, Indianapolis, IN June 1987, pages xx and xxi.

2   "Good For Business: Making Full Use of the Nation's Capital: The Environmental Scan, A Fact Finding Report of the Glass Ceiling Commission," Washington, D.C., March 1995, page 17.

3   "The Social Construction of Reverse Discrimination: The Impact of Affirmative Action on Whites," Fred L. Pincus, www.adversity.net/Pro_AA/docs/Pincus_JIR.htm.

4   www.mdcbowen.org/p2/sf/faq021.htm.

5   "Gulfstream Aerospace to Pay $2.1 million for Age Bias in EEOC Settlement, The U.S. Equal Employment Opportunity Commission, December 11, 2002.

6   op. cit., *Workforce 2000*, page 96.

7   "Remember Workforce 2000? Get Ready for Workforce 2020!", *MOSAICS: SHRM Focuses on Workplace Diversity*, Volume 3, no. 3, May/June 1997.

8   *Compensation*, 5th Edition, George T. Milkovich, Jerry M. Newman, Richard D. Irwin, A Times Mirror Higher Education Group, Inc. Company, 1996. page 505.

9   "Jury Finds Outback Steakhouse Guilty of Sex Discrimination and Illegal Retaliation: Awards Victim $2.2 million," The U.S. Equal Employment Opportunity Commission press release, September 19, 2001.

10 Statement by Susan Bianchi-Sand, Executive Director of the National Committee on Pay Equity, September 20, 1996.

11 "Little Progress on Closing Wage Gap in 2000" From: The National Committee on Pay Equity, http://feminist.com/fairpay/f_wagegap.htm.

12 "Facts on Working Women," page 7 of 11, www.dol.gov/dol/wb/public.

13 "For Female CEOs, It's Stingy at the Top," *Business Week* online, April 2001.

14 "Worth More Than We Earn: Fair Pay for Working Women," U.S. Department of Labor.

15 "It's High Time — Past Time — for Women of Color to Earn Equal Pay," AFL-CIO Fact Sheet.

16 "The Day Robert Reich became a Feminist," *The Boston Globe*, Monday, April 19, 1993, pg. 25.

17 "Male-Female Salary Gap Growing, Study Says," *The Washington Post*, January 24, 2002, A2.

18 *New Evidence on Sex Segregation and Sex Differences in Wages from Matched Employee-Employer Data*, by Kimberly Bayard, Judith Hellerstein, David Neumark, and Kenneth Troske, National Bureau of Economic Research, Inc. March 1999.

19 "Morgan Stanley Must Share Salary Data with Litigants," Colleen DeBaise, Dow Jones Newswires, www.womenonwall.com/content/article_48.shtml.

20 *Elements of Sound Base Pay Administration*, 2nd Edition. The American Compensation Association and the American Society for Personnel Administration, 1988, page 22.

21 *Legalizing Gender Inequality Courts, Markets, and Unequal Pay for Women in America*, Robert L. Nelson and William P. Bridges, Cambridge University Press, @1999, page 350-341.

22 "Poor Advancement Opportunities for Minorities," *HRMagazine*, February 1995, pages 14, 16.

23 Statistics About Business Size (including Small Business) from the U.S. Census Bureau, Table 2a. Employment Size of Employer Firms, 1999.

24 "The Alphabet Soup of Job Titles," *American Management Association International*, June 1998, by Louisa Wah, pages 40-44.

25 This number represents charges of violations of the Equal Pay Act alone, and does not include charges of multiple violations.

26 OFCCP Memo on Subject by Regional Director Joseph DuBray (undated).

27 op. cit., *Compensation*, page 279.

28 WorldatWork, *Regulatory Environments for Compensation Programs, C1*, Glossary.

29 Population Bulletin, "Women, Work and Family in America," Suzanne M. Bianchi and Daphne Spain, Population Reference Bureau, December 1996, page 24-26.

30 "Analyzing Compensation Data: A Guide to Three Approaches", U.S. Department of Labor, Employment Standards Administration, Office of Federal Contract Compliance Programs.

31 "OFCCP Cracks Down on Glass Ceiling Abuses," Lloyd Loomis, Volume 23, February-March 1999, www.hronline.org/newsltr/nwsltr299.

32 National Employment Law Institute memorandum.

33 Statement by Susan Bianchi-Sand on September 20, 1996 at the Families First Hearing.

34 op. cit., *Compensation*, page 689.

35 op. cit., *Compensation*, page 567.

36 "From Pay to Rewards: 100 Years of Change," by George T. Milkovich, Ph.D., and Jennifer Stevens, *WorldatWork Journal*, First Quarter 2000, Volume 9, Number 1, page 15.

37 "Broadbanding, Is That Your Company's Final Answer?" Michael Enos, Greg Limoges, *WorldatWork Journal*, Volume 9, Number 4, 4th Quarter 2000, page 7.

38 ibid, page 4.

39 op. cit., *Compensation*, page 286.

40 op. cit., *Compensation*, page 288.

41 "Confronting Six Myths of Broadbanding," by Kenan S. Abosch, *ACA Journal*, Autumn 1998, Volume 7, Number 3.

42 A White Paper, "A Fresh Start for Federal Pay: The Case for Modernization," April 2002, page vi.

43 Section 2301, Title 5, Merit System Principles, United States Code, Office of Personnel Management.

44 "What is Team Building, Team Building: An Introduction to the Basics", www.teamtechnology.co.uk/tt/t-articl/tb-basic.htm.

45 "Characteristics of High Performance Teams," http://cbpa.louisville.edu/skills1/High_Performance.htm.

46 op. cit., *Compensation*, page 333.

47 WorldatWork Survey, March 2000.

48 WorldatWork, Referral Bonus Survey, 2002.

49 WorldatWork, Sign-on Bonus Survey, December 2001.

50 WorldatWork, Retention Bonus Survey, May 2002.

51 WorldatWork, Spot Bonus Survey, February 2002.

52 "Getting the Pay Thing Right," *workspan*, 6/00, page 47-49.

53 "The Equity Economy: The Future is Now," *WorldatWork Journal*, Second Quarter, 2001, page 98.

54 "Qualified and Nonqualified Stock Options," Gregory Grant, www. Sexbuss.com/money.

55 "Cashless Exercising of Stock Options," Gregory Grant, www.sexbuzz.com/money.

56 Newsline, posted 5/06/02 "Companies Reassess Company Stock as Compensation."

57 op. cit., *Compensation*, pgs. 365-367.

58 op. cit., *Compensation*, page 364.

59 Newsline, posted 4/30/02 "Majority of Employees Dissatisfied with Salary Review."

60 *The Knowledge of Pay Study: Emails from the Front Line*, Paul V. Mulvey, Ph.D., Peter V. LeBlanc, CCP, Robert L. Heneman, Ph.D., Michael McInerney, May 2002.

61 op. cit., *Compensation*, page 383.

62 "Mother-friendly companies lacking" Copyright 2002, *The Tulsa World*, 5/12/02.

63 *Time Bind*, Arlie Russell Hochschild, Metropolitan Books, ©1997, pgs. 200, 201.

64 Compensation Strategy: A Guide for Senior Managers, Gerald E. Ledford, Jr., Ph.D., and Elizabeth J. Hawk, CCP, *WorldatWork Journal*, First Quarter, 2000 page 31.

65 www.dol.gov/esa/regs/compliance/ofccp/practice.htm, "Best Compensation Practices."

66 "Best Practices for Private Sector Employers, page 264, ww.eeoc.gov/task/practice.html

67 op. cit., *Pathways & Progress, Best Practices to Shatter the Glass Ceiling*, pg. 16.

68 "Fair and Square," by Marc Adams, *HR Magazine*, May 1999.

69 "Getting the Pay Thing Right," *workspan*, June 2000, Volume 43, Number 6.

70 Ibid, page 5.

71 "Piecing Together Executive Compensation," by Steve Bates, *HR Magazine*, May 2002, page 64.

72 "The Effects of Good Compensation Committee Governance" Jane T. Romweber, Hewitt Associates, LLC, *workspan*, 05/03, page 41.)

73 "Behind the Scenes: Compensation's Role in Corporate Governance," Donald D. Gallo, Myrna Hellerman, CCP, and Blair Jones, Sibson Consulting, The Segal Company, *workspan*, 05/03, page 33.

74 op. cit., page 5.

Selected References

Albelda, Randy, Drago, Robert W. and Shulman, Steven. (August 1, 2001). "Unlevel Playing Fields: Understanding Wage Inequality and Discrimination." *Dollars & Sense*. Book.ISBN: 1878585207.

Altman, Daniel. (September 8, 2002). "How to Tie Pay To Goals, Instead of the Stock Price." *The New York Times*. Section 3, pg. 4, Col. 1.

Anonymous. (2001). "Pay Equity: A New Approach Needed." *The Worklife Report*. 13(2): 4-6.

Anonymous. (February 15, 2001). "Rights Commission Seeks Agency to Monitor Pay Equity." *The Star Phoenix* (Saskatoon). National, pg. B7.

Anonymous. (April 19, 2001). "You Need to Know About These Affirmative Action Changes." *HR On Campus*, LRP Publications. 4(4).

Anonymous. (June 2001). "Pay Equity Comes to British Columbia." *Human Resources Advisor Newsletter* (Western Edition), pgs. 1-2.

Anonymous. (June 13, 2001). "CWA Urges Prompt Passage of Paycheck Fairness Act." *PR Newswire*. Washington Dateline.

Anonymous. (December 23, 2001). "A Disturbing Disparity." News and Observer. *Business Work & Money*. pg. E1.

Anonymous. (March 31, 2002). "To Shrink the Pay Gap, Turn Up the Volume." *The New York Times*, Section 3, pg. 9.

Anonymous. (August 2003). "11 Quick Fixes to Problems With Your Staff Pay Plan." Compensation & Benefits for Law Offices, pg. 2.

Armour, Stephanie. (January 10, 2001). "Bias Suits Put Spotlight on Workplace Diversity Critics Cite Lucrative Fees." *USA Today*. Money, pg. 18.

Blau, Francine D. and Lawrence M. Kahn. (Fall 2000). "Gender Differences in Pay." *Journal of Economic Perspectives*. 14(4): 75-99.

Bloomberg News & Wire. (May 29, 2002). "Coca-Cola Co. Will Pay $8.1 Million in Back Compensation to 2,178 Former and Current Employees After a Federal Agency and the Company Found the Workers Were Underpaid." *Bloomberg Business*, pg. 3D.

Brown, Tim. (February 2003). "Building the Case for Salary Surveys in Tight Times." *workspan*. 46(2): 42-45.

Chaudhuri, Ananda and Kathleen Collins. (July/August 2000). "The 2000 Salary Survey." *Working Woman*. 25(7): 58-63.

Dauphinee, Kate. (Third Quarter 2001). "Reader's Perspective: Taking Competencies to the Next Level? They've Already Arrived. *WorldatWork Journal*. 10(3): 6-7.

Ellig, Bruce R., SPHR. (Third Quarter 2000). "CEO Pay – A 20th Century Review." *WorldatWork Journal*. 9(3): 71-78.

Fay, Charles and Howard Risher. (July 2000). "New OFCCP Survey: Comparable Worth Redux?" *workspan*. 43(7): 41-44.

Farrell, Christopher. (August 9, 1999). "Women in the Workplace: Is Parity Finally in Sight?" *Business Week*.

Fay, Charles, Ph.D., CCP and Risher, Howard, Ph.D. (July 2000). "New OFCCP Survey: Comparable Worth Redux?" *workspan*. 43(7):41-44.

Figart, Deborah M. (March 2000). "Equal Pay for Equal Work: The Role of Job Evaluation in an Evolving Social Norm." *Journal of Economic Issues*. 34(1) 1-20.

Garza, Irasema T. (June 9, 2000). "Ten Steps to an Equal Pay Self-Audit for Employers." *U.S. Department of Labor*. http://www.dol.gov/dol/wb/10step71.htm

Garza, Irasema T. (June 9, 2000). "Tools for Employers, Making Equal Pay a Reality in Your Workplace." Facts on Working Women, *U.S. Department of Labor*. http://www.dol.gov/wb/public/we_pubs/tools.htm

Gerencher, Kristen. (August 14, 2002). "Fighting the Pay Gap Requires Careful Approach." *CBS MarketWatch*. Personal Finance Gender Gap.

Gulane, Judy T. (August 29, 2003). "Substandard Working Conditions." *Business World*. pg. 25.

Howe, Polly. (April 14, 2003). "Women in the Red Demand Equal Pay Laws." *PR Newswire*. Financial News.

Heneman, Robert L., Ph.D. (Third Quarter 2001). "Work Evaluation: Current State of the Art and Future Prospects." *WorldatWork Journal*. 10(3): 65-70.

Koechel, Jane F., CCP. (January 2001). "Free Agent Syndrome Fueling Turnover Frenzy." *workspan*. 44(1): 6-8.

Latta, Geoffrey W. and Cummins, Siobhan E. (September 1999). "Policy Considerations in Localizing Expatriates." *ACA News*. 42(8): 36-38.

Mannila, Charles, CCP. (March 2001). "Steering Clear of Court." *workspan*. 44(3): 56-59.

McCann, Michael W. (July 1994). *Rights at Work: Pay Equity Reform and the Politics of Legal Mobilization*. University of Chicago Press. Book. ISBN: 0226555720.

Mohler, Katy M. and Stillson, Cori A. (First Quarter 2001). "History Still in the Making: The Continuing Struggle for Equal Pay." *WorldatWork Journal*. 10(1): 28-37.

Nelson, Robert L. and Bridges, William. (May 1999). *Legalizing Gender Inequality: Courts, Markets and Unequal Pay for Women in America*. Cambridge University Press. Book. ISBN: 0521627508.

Nielsen, Niels H. (Third Quarter 2002). "Job Content Evaluation Techniques Based on Marxian Economics." *WorldatWork Journal*. 11(3): 52-62.

Pinkley, Robin L. and Northcraft, Gregory B. (March 2000). *Get Paid What You're Worth: The Expert Negotiator's Guide to Salary and Compensation*. St. Martin's Press. Book. ISBN: 0312242549.

Posnak, Diane D. (July/August 1999). "A Road Map to Changes in Directors' Pay." *ACA News*. 42(7): 37-39.

Rahbar-Daniels, Dana, Erickson, Mary Lou and Dalik, Arden. (First Quarter 2001). "Here to Stay: Taking Competencies to the Next Level." *WorldatWork Journal*. 10(1): 70-77.

Rankin, Adam. (September 9, 2003). "Closer to Unveiling a Solution to the Pay Gap Between Female and Hispanic Workers and Their White Male Counterparts." *Albuquerque Journal* (NM). Journal North. pg. 1.

Scott, K. Dow, Ph.D.; Morajda, Dennis, MSOD and Bishop, James W. (First Quarter 2002). "Increase Company Competitiveness — Tune Up Your Pay System." *WorldatWork Journal*. 11(1): 35-42.

Stokes, Douglas M., Ph.D., and Pittel, Mark E., CCP. (Third Quarter 2003). "Auditing Payroll Data for OFCCP Compliance." *WorldatWork Journal.* 12(3): 6-13.

Trevor, Charlie and Graham, Mary E. (Fourth Quarter 2000). "Deriving the Market Wage." *WorldatWork Journal,* 9(4): 69-76.

Vecchio, Robert P. (December 2002). "Leadership and Gender Advantage." *The Leadership Quarterly.* Vol. 13, No. 6.

Weeks, Sandra. (Fourth Quarter 2002). "Reader's Perspective: Job Evaluation is Alive and Well ... at Least in Canada." *WorldatWork Journal.*11(4):10-13.

Wilde, Candee. (June 12, 2000.) "Women in IT Strive for Equal Job Compensation." *Information Week.* 790: 226-228.